PRETTY PETALS

More Fantastical Designs

By Sheri Howard

PRETTY PETALS

More Fantastical Designs

By Sheri Howard

Editor: Kent Richards
Technical Editor: Jane Miller
Book Design: Bob Deck
Photography: Aaron Leimkuehler
Illustration: Eric Sears
Production Assistance: Jo Ann Groves

Website: sherimhoward.blogspot.com

Published by:
Kansas City Star Books
1729 Grand Blvd.
Kansas City, Missouri, USA 64108

First edition, first printing
ISBN: 978-1-61169-039-2

Library of Congress Control Number:
2012933023

Printed in the United States of America by Walsworth Publishing Co., Marceline, MO
To order copies, call StarInfo at (816) 234-4636 and say "Books."

Table of Contents

Introduction

The Pretty Petal quilt designs started out as sketches I drew while traveling and evolved into flowers that I thought would make a beautiful quilt. A lot of memories about flowers came back to me while writing this book. I was quite surprised at just how many memories I had that included flowers. I love that flowers are all so unique. I love that their colors and scents are so distinctive. I love the way that the colors in a flower flow from light to dark and from one color into another. I think they are WONDERFUL! It is such a delight to write a quilt book about flowers!

When I was thinking about the colors I wanted to use to make the Pretty Petals quilt, I wanted colors that were cheerful and bright. This started me thinking about how I feel about color and where my love of color came from.

I went to grade school in the 1960's and I remember my first box of 24 count crayons. A few years later, perhaps 5th or 6th grade, we were old enough to have a box of water color paints. Some of you may remember that the Prang® water colors came in a black tin box. I loved that little tin box of color–it represented a time of exploration, and artistic creations. I grew up in a time when art was an important part of school and our grade school was no exception. We had regular art days and art projects.

I think of those color crayons and Prang® colors as pure colors. They are the true primary and secondary colors I learned about in art class, and those are the colors I wanted to use for the quilts in this book. It was an adventure looking for those pure colors in fabrics and I envisioned them making the brightest, most cheerful and

imaginary flowers for my quilt. I like to use small prints or fabrics with just two colors in the small prints—that way the colors are the important part, not the pattern. I think you will find it easy to find pure colors in your fabric shop as they are good staples. Take a 24 count box of crayons to the store if you need help with choosing colors.

I am crazy about those twisty, swirly flower stems, but this does pose a challenge for the freezer paper appliqué method, so I did use fusible web appliqué in this book. These stems would be fun if you had the time to do needle turn appliqué but use the appliqué method you like best. For fusible web appliqué, I like to use YLI® brand of monofilament thread—I used the smoke color. There are many kinds of monofilament threads, find one that is not too thick and that works well with your sewing machine.

Ralph Waldo Emerson said, *"Earth laughs in flowers."* I agree.

I hope you enjoy the pretty petals!

Sheri

"With a few flowers in my garden, half a dozen pictures and some books, I live without envy."

Lope de Vega

Dedication

This book is dedicated first to a woman I scarcely knew—Mrs. Hicks. She had a wonderful flower garden that bordered her entire back yard. Her house was almost exactly in the middle of the block between my house and my friend Cathy's house in Boise, Idaho. We would walk by her garden–back and forth–many times a day during the summer months, and I remember her kneeling over her flowers working in her flower beds. If Mrs. Hicks was working near the sidewalk we would stop and talk with her, and sometimes she would cut a flower for Cathy and me to take with us along our way. I loved her flower gardens.

Lastly, this book is dedicated to all those who grow (or did grow) flowers that made a lasting impression on my memory.

"And beauty is not a need but an ecstasy.
It is not a mouth thirsting nor an empty hand stretched forth,
But rather a heart enflamed and a soul enchanted.
It is not the image you would see nor the song you would hear,
But rather an image you see though you close your eyes
and a song you hear though you shut your ears.
It is not the sap within the furrowed bark, nor a wing attached to a claw,
But rather a garden forever in bloom and a flock of angels forever in flight."

Kahlil Gibran - "Beauty"

PRETTY PETALS

PRETTY PETALS QUILT
Finished size: 88" x 112"
Designed by Sheri Howard
Quilted by Sheri Bear of Bear's Custom Quilting

The flowers for this quilt started out as sketches drawn while I traveled. They needed a name for easier identification for you the quilter, so I tried to envision what flower they could represent. These flower blocks are an imaginary play on common everyday flowers and could be named most anything. You will see that they are named to match some of my flower memories. Their shapes may look like flowers you know and may even summon a memory of your own.

BLOCK 1
Sweet Pea

My mom planted a lot of sweet peas. She would soak the little seeds in a bowl of water the night before planting to help give them a head start in sprouting. My mom said the more you picked them, the more they would produce flowers. So we would pick them quite often and kept little bouquets in a glass in the kitchen. Sweet peas are one of those flowers that smell so wonderful—I loved all the pastel colors mixed together growing up the garden fence.

Did you ever grow sweet pea flowers? Who do you know that did?

BLOCK 2
Marigold

One year at the end of summer, my dad and I picked the dried marigolds and saved them in a white envelope to use for next year's seeds. I didn't like the smell of marigolds when I was young, but now they bring happy thoughts of a more quiet time—a time of no worries, and endless summer days and nights. As I got older

I was surprised to find out that there were so many different varieties of marigolds.

How many different varieties of marigolds do you have in your garden?

BLOCK 3
Daisy

A few years ago I drove by someone's house and in their flower garden was something that looked like a daisy, but it was not white. Several days later I stopped and walked over to see what it was. Yes, it was a daisy and it wasn't white! It was a pretty pink-purplish color. I didn't even know colored daisies existed—I had to find out where to get some. Where had I been all these years? So of course the next year at the nursery I inquired about them and purchased some for my own flower garden. They make me smile when I see them!

Do you have colored daisies, do you know someone who does? Have you seen them in any other color?

BLOCK 4
Zinnia

I have a wonderful childhood memory of the zinnias that grew on the west side of our house. I must have been pretty young as they were very tall—as tall as me! I distinctively remember standing there measuring the flowers to my height.

What is one of your first recollections of flowers?

BLOCK 5
Rose

I have always loved flowers. Isn't it interesting that every flower has its own distinct smell? When I lived in Boise, Idaho, we had a white rose bush on the corner of our yard very near the street. They had the softest pink centers with really large flowers and had a wonderful aroma. Even now, if there are roses near the sidewalk when I go walking, I love to stop and smell the roses in people's flower gardens—they all smell so delightfully different.

What was the first time you smelled a rose? What rose is your favorite?

BLOCK 6
Poppy

Growing up, we had orange poppies that grew in our back yard flower garden. They eventually spread everywhere and were over taking the flower garden, so one day my dad finally dug them all out. I thought the little pods that were left when the petals fell off were so intriguing, it always seemed so sad that you couldn't use them for something fun. My favorite color of poppy is red.

Do you have memories of poppies in someone's garden? What is your favorite color?

Bleeding Heart

Mrs. Lanager was our next door neighbor in Boise, Idaho. On the west side of her house was a bleeding heart flower bush. Our houses were quite close, (about two swipes with the lawn mower close) and we did not have a bleeding heart bush. I loved to go and look at Mrs. Lanager's bush and thought the flowers were SO wonderful. How could a little flower grow just like a little heart? I did see a white bleeding heart bush once but it wasn't nearly as pretty as the pink one.

Who do you know that had a bleeding heart bush? Have you ever seen a white one?

BLOCK 8

Geranium

I don't know where I was when I smelled a geranium, but I do remember NOT liking it. Even the leaves smell like geraniums. They don't bother me now, and I LOVE the darkest red ones. One year when I went to the local nursery to pick out my spring flowers, they had the most beautiful deep "pure" red geraniums. Of course I bought those for my flower pots. I have never seen that color since.

Do you like the smell of a geranium? What color do you buy?

BLOCK 9
Sunflower

I was surprised when I heard that sunflowers follow the sun. I had never heard of such a thing, but it is true. (You can Google it yourself.) The phenomena is called positive phototropism—a very fancy name, but fascinating all the same! One year we grew the really big ones that had seeds you could cook and eat. How delightful, a flower that has seeds you can eat!

Did you ever grow those really tall sunflowers? Did you cook and eat them?

BLOCK 10
Iris

This past spring, a woman in our town told me her iris garden had over 95 varieties. I was intrigued, so my husband and I drove out to her house and had a little tour. She showed us all the different kinds and spoke about each one like it was one of her children. Many were world class and some had even won national awards. She had little sticks by each variety with its name and what year it was made famous. They were so fragrant—what a lovely iris garden!

Who do you know that has irises in their garden? What varieties do they have?

Snapdragon

I remember having snapdragons in our flower garden at home and in my grandma's flower garden too. It was so fun to pick off the little flowers and snap them open and closed. It's an amazing thing when you think about it—how these flowers can snap open and closed!

Did you ever pick snapdragon flowers and pinch them open and closed? Have you ever seen an orange snapdragon? I have!

BLOCK 12
Carnation

I love how pink carnations look and smell. Perhaps because they were in several of the prom corsages I had while in high school. Oh those were the days...a prom, a boy, a dress and a corsage!

Who was your first prom flower from? What was your favorite prom corsage and who was it from?

Fabric Requirements

Aqua or blue gingham background: 8 yards
Dark aqua for corners: 3 yards
Spring green for cornerstones: ¼ yard

APPLIQUÉ FABRIC:
2 reds: ⅓ yard each
2 yellows: fat quarter or ¼ yard each
1 brown: ⅛ yard
1 purple: ⅛ yard
1 royal blue: ⅛ yard, plus ⅞ yard for binding
1 medium blue: fat quarter or ¼ yard
1 spring green: ½ yard, (can be the same green
  as cornerstones)
1 light green: fat quarter or ¼ yard
2 medium greens: ⅓ yard each
2 oranges: fat quarter or ¼ yard each
4 yards fusible web

*"The artist is the
confidant of nature,
flowers carry on dialogues
with him through the graceful
bending of their stems
and the harmoniously tinted
nuances of their blossoms.
Every flower has a cordial word
which nature directs towards him."*

Auguste Rodin

Tip Invest in a 15" square ruler, you will be
glad you did.

Sewing Instructions

All seams ¼" unless otherwise stated.

FOR APPLIQUÉ BLOCKS:
From aqua gingham cut:
12 – 15" squares

Tip Spray squares lightly with Mary Ellen's Best Press® spray starch and press. I like this spray because it is very light and does not leave a residue. This will help keep your fabric flat and straight while you appliqué.

1. Trace each block's appliqué using templates on pages 66–89, following colors from photo. If you trace the largest pieces first, you can use the smaller bits of fusible web for the smallest pieces. I worked on one block at a time to keep from getting all those small pieces mixed up.

Tip I used a dime, nickel and quarter for the smaller circles, also spools, lids, and small dishes for the larger circles. Use what you have to trace the circles on the fusible web—it makes for easier tracing and cutting!

Tip I save the little bits of fusible web and store them in a zip lock bag to use on the smaller templates.

2. Fold the 15" square in half diagonally and lightly press with an iron so you have a point of reference to place the stem and other appliqués. Place the stem and other appliqué pieces along pressed fold.

3. Place the stem on the block background first. Place it ¼" from both sides of the bottom corner, so when you sew on the dark aqua corner pieces your stem is exactly in the middle. See diagram 1.

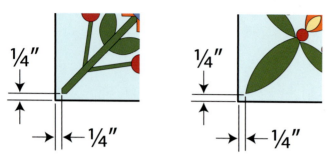

diagram 1

4. Lay the large pieces of the appliqué on top of the stem. Place the appliqué pieces on in layers, press and appliqué each layer. Cut away any background fabric from the back to eliminate bulk.

5. It's IMPORTANT to press the block between appliqué layers to keep block and appliqué lying as flat as possible. If using monofilament thread, BE CAREFUL to not over heat. The thread WILL melt! I like to lightly spray my block again after all the appliqué is on and press well.

6. TRIM blocks to measure 14 ½". This is where the 15" ruler will be SO helpful. Make sure you leave ¼" at the corners for the points of your stems.

DARK AQUA CORNERS:
From dark aqua fabric cut:
24 – 11 ¼" squares.
Subcut once diagonally creating 48 corner triangles. See diagram 2.

diagram 2

Tip Spray the long edges of the triangles with fabric spray starch and press to help minimize stretching, as you are sewing along the bias with these triangles.

1. Mark the center of the long edge of triangle, and the center of one side of 14 ½" appliquéd blocks. Pin together at center mark. Pin along entire length of long side of triangle starting at the middle and working out to the ends. See diagram 3. Pinning will help keep your blocks and corners from stretching out of shape, this is important! There will be a little extra length at the ends for future trimming. (Nothing I hate more than not having enough fabric to trim!) Sew opposite sides of the 14 ½" block with dark aqua corners. Press seams toward dark aqua corner. See diagram 3. Pin and sew remaining two sides of block with dark aqua corner triangles. Press toward dark aqua corner.

"Flowers always make people better, happier, and more helpful, they are sunshine, food and medicine for the soul."

Luther Burbank

diagram 3

2. Trim blocks to 20 ¼" square. Make sure you leave a ¼" seam allowance around the entire block. See diagram 4. Repeat for all 12 blocks.

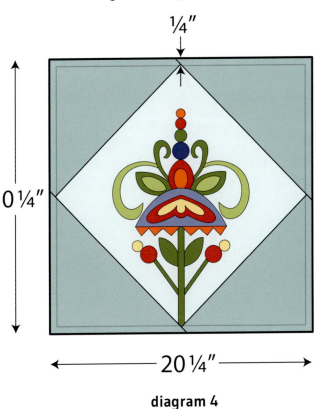

¼"

0 ¼"

20 ¼"

diagram 4

SASHING:
From aqua gingham cut:
16 strips – 3 ½" WOF (width of fabric)
Subcut 31 – 3 ½" x 20 ¼" strips

From spring green cut:
2 strips – 3 ½" WOF
Subcut 20 – 3 ½" squares

BORDERS:
From aqua gingham cut:
11 – 9 ½" strips WOF. Sew together end to end. You will cut exact lengths later.

"Happiness held is the seed;
Happiness shared is the flower."

John Harrigan

CONSTRUCTING QUILT CENTER

1. Lay out blocks in the order that makes you happy.

2. Sew 1 – 3 1/2" x 20 1/4" aqua gingham sashing strip to left side of all 12 blocks. See diagram 5.

diagram 5

3. Sew blocks and sashing together to make row of 3 blocks. See diagram 6. Repeat for all 4 rows.

diagram 6

4. Add 1 – 3 1/2" x 20 1/4" aqua gingham sashing strip to right side of all 4 rows. See diagram 7.

diagram 7

5. Sew 4 – 3 1/2" x 3 1/2" spring green squares to ends of 3 – 3 1/2" x 20 1/4" aqua gingham sashing strips. See diagram 8. Make 5 strips.

diagram 8

6. Sew strips to top of each block row. See diagram 9. Repeat for all 4 rows.

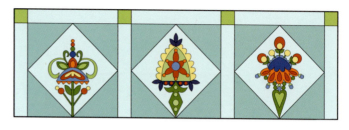

diagram 9

7. Sew last strip row to bottom of row 4. See diagram 10.

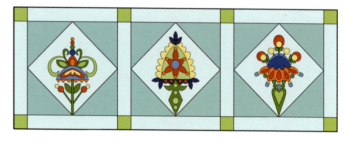

diagram 10

8. Sew rows together to complete quilt center. See diagram 11.

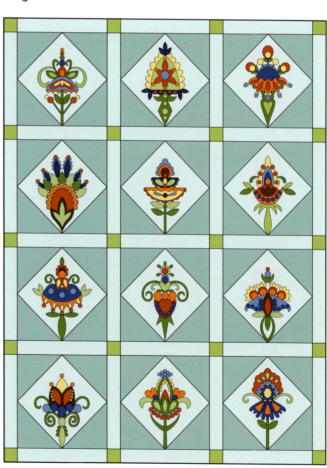

diagram 11

BORDER SIDES:

Tip Measure quilt center length in 3 places. Average these measurements together to determine quilt center length or width. (All quilts will differ slightly, as not all $1/4$" seams are the same.) See diagram 12.

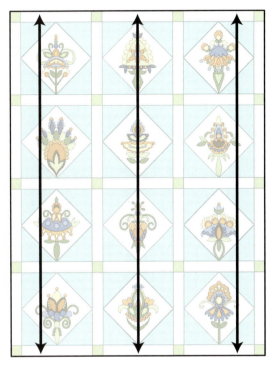

diagram 12

1. Cut 2 – 9 $1/2$" border strips 2" longer than the length of your quilt center measurement to allow for slight shrinking from appliqué. You will trim to exact measurements later.

Tip Spray border strips lightly with fabric starch and press before appliquéing.

2. Mark the center of the border strip. Lay appliqué pieces on border strip and press, making sure you tuck the swirly stems under the larger pieces. Appliqué larger pieces first, then place the other appliqué pieces on layers and appliqué as you go. See diagram 14 for placement of pieces for side borders.

3. Press appliqué well, lightly spraying with fabric spray starch and press after each appliqué design. This helps keep the border fabric straight.

4. Trim borders to 8 $1/2$" width. Cut $1/4$" from the top and $1/4$" from the bottom of border strip. DO NOT cut $1/2$" from only one side. Then cut from both ends of the border strips to the measurement of your quilt center length from diagram 12.

5. Mark center of border strip. Mark center of the sides of the quilt center. Pin centers right sides together and continue to pin the entire border to the quilt center before you begin to sew. (This keeps your borders from becoming longer than your quilt.)

6. Sew borders to both sides of quilt center, see diagram 16, making sure the design is facing the correct way! Check the photo for the direction. Press seams toward borders.

Side border

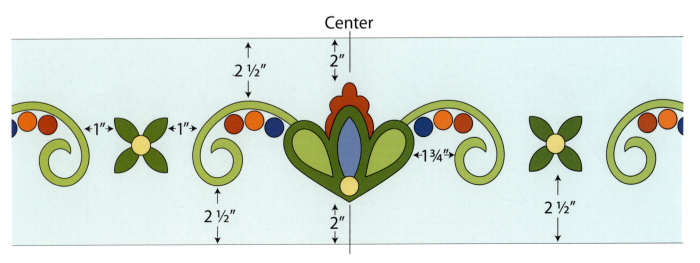

diagram 14

BORDERS TOP AND BOTTOM:

1. Repeat measuring of quilt center for top and bottom of quilt as in TIP for quilt length. See diagram 13. Repeat all the border steps for top and bottom, same as for border sides. See diagram 15 for placement of pieces for top and bottom borders.

2. Press appliqué well, lightly spraying with fabric spray starch and press after each appliqué design. This helps keep the border fabric straight.

3. Trim borders to 8 ½" width. Cut ¼" from the top and ¼" from the bottom of border strip. DO NOT cut ½" from only one side. Then cut from both ends of border strips to fit your measurement the quilt center width from diagram 13.

4. Mark center of border strip. Mark the center of the top and bottom of quilt center. Pin centers right sides together and continue to pin entire border to the quilt center before you begin to sew.

5. Sew borders to top and bottom of quilt center, making sure the design is facing the correct way! See diagram 16. (I placed the top border to face toward the end of the bed so it faces the same way as the bottom border.) Check the photo for the direction. Press seams toward borders.

QUILT and ENJOY!

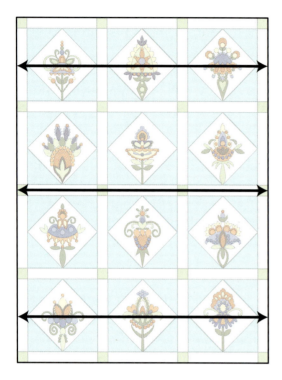

diagram 13

Top - bottom border

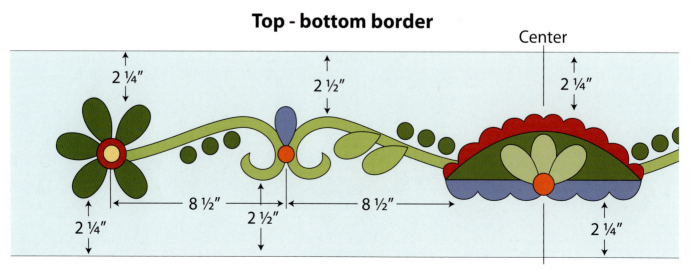

diagram 15

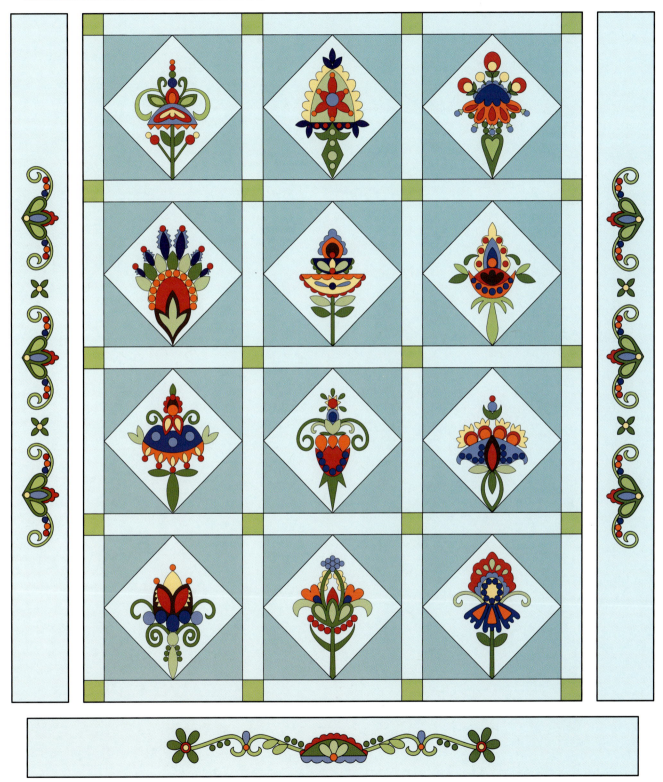

diagram 16

EURO PILLOW SHAMS

EURO PILLOW SHAMS
Finished size: 24" x 24"
Designed by Sheri Howard
Quilted by Sheri Bear of Bear's Custom Quilting

Have you ever made a quilt but didn't have any pretty pillows to use with it? OR have you had pretty pillows but they covered up the pretty quilt? Me too! I have designed these euro shams to fit on top of your quilt, so all the blocks will show. I made two for my full size bed, but on a queen or king size bed, you may want three.

Fabric Requirements
(makes 2 shams)

Aqua or blue gingham: 2 ¼ yard
Dark aqua for corners: ⅓ yard
Light green: ⅛ yard
2 yards muslin - backing for quilting the sham top
2 – 30" pieces of thin batting
1 yard fusible web
2 – 24" pillow forms

"To be overcome by the fragrance of flowers is a delectable form of defeat."

Beverly Nichols

Sewing Instructions
All seams are ¼" unless otherwise stated.

PILLOW SHAM:
From aqua gingham cut:
2 – 15" squares.

> **Tip** Spray squares lightly with fabric spray starch and press.

1. Trace the block's appliqué that match the top right and top left blocks of your quilt. (This way, when the shams are on the bed, all the blocks of the quilt will show.) Use templates from the Pretty Petals quilt blocks and follow the colors from your quilt. If you trace the largest pieces first, you can use the smaller bits of fusible web for the smallest pieces.

2. Fold the 15" square in half diagonally and lightly press with an iron so you have a point of reference to place the stem and other appliqués. Place the stem and other appliqué pieces along the pressed fold.

3. Place the stem on the block background first. Place it ¼" from both sides of the bottom corner, so when you sew the dark aqua corner pieces your stem is exactly in the middle. See diagram 1 from Pretty Petals quilt instructions.

4. Lay the large pieces of the appliqué on top of the stem. Place other pieces of appliqué that will be under the top layers, press and appliqué. (Like stems.) Cut away any background fabric from the back to eliminate bulk. Place the appliqué pieces on in layers, press and appliqué each layer.

5. It's IMPORTANT to press block between appliqué layers to keep block and appliqué lying as flat as possible. If using monofilament thread, BE CAREFUL to not over heat. The thread WILL melt! I like to lightly spray my block again after all the appliqué is on and press well.

6. TRIM blocks to measure 14 ½". This is where the 15" ruler will be SO helpful. Make sure you leave ¼" at the corners for the points of your stems.

DARK AQUA CORNERS:
From dark aqua fabric cut:
4 – 11 1/2" squares.
Subcut once diagonally creating 8 corner triangles. See diagram 2 from Pretty Petals quilt instructions.

> **Tip** Spray the long edges of the triangles with fabric spray starch and press to help minimize stretching, as you are sewing along the bias with these triangles.

1. Mark the center of the long edge of triangle, and the center of one side of 14 1/2" appliquéd blocks. Pin together at center mark. Pin along entire length of long side of triangle starting at the middle and working out to the ends. Pinning will help keep your blocks and corners from stretching out of shape, this is important! There will be a little extra length at the ends for future trimming. (Nothing I hate more than not having enough fabric to trim!) Sew opposite sides of the 14 1/2" block with dark aqua corners. Press seams toward dark aqua corner. See diagram 3 from Pretty Petals quilt instructions. Pin and sew remaining two sides of block with dark aqua corner triangles. Press toward dark aqua corner.

2. Trim blocks to 20 1/4" square. Make sure you leave a 1/4" seam allowance around the entire block. See diagram 4 for Pretty Petals quilt. Repeat for both shams.

SASHING:
From aqua gingham cut:
4 – 3 1/2" strips WOF (width of fabric)
Subcut 8 – 3 1/2" x 20 1/4" strips

From light green cut:
1 – 3 1/2" strip WOF
Subcut 8 – 3 1/2" squares

CONSTRUCTING SHAMS:
1. Sew 1 – 3 1/2" x 20 1/4" aqua gingham sashing strip to both sides of appliquéd block. See diagram 1.

diagram 1

2. Sew 1 – 3 1/2" x 3 1/2" light green square to each end of 2 – 3 1/2" x 20 1/4" aqua gingham sashing strips. See diagram 2.

diagram 2

3. Sew sashing strip with green blocks to top and bottom of sham. See diagram 3.

diagram 3

"Where flowers bloom so does hope."

Lady Bird Johnson

QUILT THE SHAM TOP:

Layer sham top with a piece of batting and muslin. Quilt to match your quilt. Trim shams to 24 ½" square.

SHAM BACKS:

From aqua gingham cut:
1 – 15" x 24 ½"
1 – 18" x 24 ½"

1. Stitch a narrow hem along one 24 ½" side of each piece. See diagram 4 and 5.

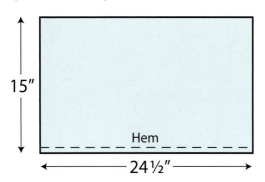

diagram 4

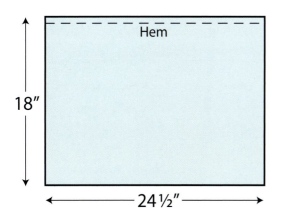

diagram 5

2. Lay 15" x 24 ½" on top of 18" x 24 ½" piece, overlapping pieces, right sides up. Making the back piece to measure 24 ½" x 24 ½". See diagram 6. Pin pieces together.

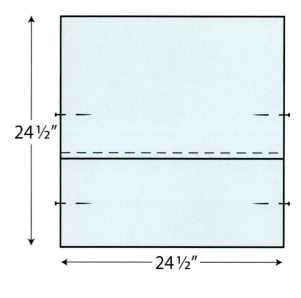

diagram 6

3. Lay quilted sham top on the back, right sides together. Sew around entire 24 ½" square, back stitching where back pieces overlap for extra security when pillow form is inserted. Trim corners.

4. Turn sham inside out, press. Top stitch around entire sham ¼" from outside edge.

5. Insert pillow form.

"Bread feeds the body, indeed, but flowers feed also the soul."

The Koran

FRILLY PILLOW CASE

FRILLY PILLOW CASE
Finished size: 20" x 30"
Designed by Sheri Howard

When I was thinking about using the Pretty Petals quilt on my bed, I thought of how cheerful I would feel getting into bed with special pillow cases—something "pretty and frilly." They would have to match the quilt of course, be washable, but be a bit whimsical! My husband may not want to sleep on one, but I will! Sweet dreams.

Fabric Requirements

FOR 1 QUEEN SIZE PILLOW CASE:
Aqua or blue gingham: $3/4$ yard
White with dots: $2/3$ yard
1 package store bought piping, any color.
Royal blue: 1 strip – $1\,1/4$" x 42" (To cover piping.)
Royal blue thread or thread to match piping strip
Crochet thread (optional for gathering ruffle)

Cutting Instructions

Seams allowances are $1/2$" unless otherwise stated.

From aqua gingham cut:
1 - 26" x 41"

From white with dots cut:
2 - 12" x WOF (width of fabric)

Sewing Instructions

1. Fold aqua gingham right sides together. Sew down the long side and along one short side, using a ½" seam. (I think a ½" seam will make the seams more stable where the pillow case will get a lot of use.) Clip corners.

2. Sew white with dots 12" ruffle strips together end to end to form a circle.

3. Fold white with dots ruffle in half lengthwise, wrong sides together and press.

4. Gather along the raw edge.

GATHERING:

This is the method of gathering I use on a long piece of fabric:

1. For this project: Cut 2 pieces of crochet thread 50" long.

2. Divide the ruffle in half. Mark halves with a pin. Mark the aqua gingham pillow case in halves with pins.

3. On the side with the raw edge, start the crochet thread at the pin marker, lay the crochet thread on the ruffle about ¼" from the edge (where you would normally do a machine gathering stitch), leaving a 5" tail of crochet thread from the beginning. See diagram 1. You are only gathering one half of the ruffle at a time.

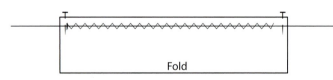

Fold

diagram 1

4. Using a wide zig-zag, sew back and forth ACROSS the crochet thread, do not catch the crochet with your sewing stitches. Back stitch at the beginning to secure zig-zag, as you will be pulling the crochet thread to gather and you want the zig-zags to stay in place.

5. Sew across the crochet thread until you get to the halfway pin. Back stitch at the halfway pin to secure zig-zag. Cut zig-zag thread. Leave in the pins at the halfway marks.

6. Repeat for other side of ruffle. Don't pull the gathering yet. Set ruffle aside.

PIPING:

1. Measure your aqua gingham pillow case opening precisely. This is the measurement you will cut your piping.

2. Cut the piping the exact measurement of the aqua gingham opening. You do not need a seam allowance for this piping, as we are going to butt the ends together.

3. Cut the 1 ¼" royal blue strip ½" longer than the cut piping. Sew ends together to form a circle using a ¼" seam allowance. Press seam open.

4. Leave the original colored fabric on the piping. Lay the piping on the royal blue piece, fold over and begin sewing along the same seam as the original piping, using royal blue thread. Basically, you are just covering the piping, making your own color. Butt the ends of the piping together as you sew to form a circle.

"God has sown his name on the heavens in glittering stars; but on earth he planteth his name by tender flowers."

Jean Paul Richter

ATTACHING PIPING AND RUFFLE:

1. Pin the royal blue piping to the right side of the aqua gingham part of the pillow case. Sew from the piping side along the exact stitching of the piping which you just covered. This way blue stitching thread will not show. Sew around entire circle.

2. Pin the ruffle on the pillowcase, put the halfway pins on the side seams. One pin should be at the long side seam, and one at the halfway around the pillow case opening. (As there is only one side seam.)

3. You will be gathering and sewing only one side of the ruffle onto the pillowcase at a time. Now, pull the gathering strings from each end until the gathers are the same size as half of the pillow case, wrapping the crochet thread around the pins a couple of times in a figure-eight. See diagram 2. (This will hold the gathering threads.) Pin gather to right side of the pillow case, adjusting gathers as you go.

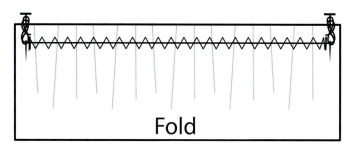

Fold

diagram 2

4. Hold the figure-eight threads out of the way as your sew.

5. Sew the first half of the ruffle to the pillow case.

Tip I stitch the ruffle to the pillow case from the pillow case side, not on the gathers as you would think, so I can sew on the same stitches where I sewed the piping onto the pillowcase. You have to be careful and make sure your gathers stay nice and flat. This way, the stitching from the piping does not show when I turn the pillowcase inside out because I have sewn on the same stitching.

6. Repeat the gathering of the other side of the pillowcase same as instructions 2–5.

7. Turn pillow case inside out. Make sure all your gathers look nice before you pull out the crochet thread. IF you like how your gathers look cut the crochet thread and gently pull it out.

FINISHING:

1. Finish raw edge of the seam using a zig-zag or serger. Finish all the layers at one time.

2. Clip corners.

3. Press pillowcase.

4. Top stitch on the right side of the pillow case along the piping, sewing through the entire seam. This will keep the seam lying flat.

ENJOY sleeping on your frilly pillow case!

"If you've never been thrilled to the very edges of your soul by a flower in spring bloom, maybe your soul has never been in bloom."

Terri Guillemets

KALEIDOSCOPE QUILT

KALEIDOSCOPE QUILT
Finished size: 52" x 52"
Designed by Sheri Howard
Quilted by Susan Hansen of Suzy Q's Quilts

I don't know how old I was, but I have a vivid memory of the first time I saw a kaleidoscope. Me, my mom, her friend Shirley Packham and Shirley's girls were at a thrift sale in downtown Boise, Idaho. There I happened upon a kaleidoscope and I remember how mesmerized I was by it. To this day, if I ever see one in a store, I ALWAYS pick them up and look at the incredible shapes they produce. They still amaze me!

Originally this book was to be about an entire quilt of these kaleidoscope blocks, however they were so small and detailed that I only made one block! I liked how they looked all put together to make a kaleidoscope, so I enlarged them to the present size and made one quilt, with one block. The appealing thing is you can choose any block from the Pretty Petals quilt and make the kaleidoscope of your choice.

Fabric Requirements

Cream print for background: 7/8 yard
Light green: 1/3 yard
Medium blue: 2/3 yard
Blue floral: 1 1/4 yard

APPLIQUÉ FABRIC:
Medium blue: 4" x 15"
Bright yellow: 7" x 18"
Medium green: fat quarter
Dark chocolate brown: fat quarter
Bright red: 10" x 18"
1 yard fusible web

Cutting Instructions
All seams are 1/4" unless otherwise stated

From cream print cut:
4 - 15" squares

BORDERS:
From light green cut:
4 – 2 1/2" strips WOF (width of fabric)
Subcut:
2 – 28 1/2" strips
2 – 32 1/2" strips

From medium blue cut:
4 – 4 1/2" strips WOF
Subcut:
2 – 32 1/2" strips
2 – 40 1/2" strips

From blue floral cut:
6 – 6 1/2" strips WOF
Subcut:
2 – 40 1/2" strips
2 – 52 1/2" strips

APPLIQUÉ PIECES:
Cut pieces for appliqué block 4 times

Sewing Instructions

Tip Spray squares lightly with Mary Ellen's Best Press® spray starch and press. I like this spray because it is very light and does not leave a residue. This will help keep your fabric flat and straight while you appliqué .

1. Trace the iris block appliqué using templates on pages 84–85. Be sure if you are using fusible web that you trace both sides of flowers, and stems. If you trace the largest pieces first, you can use the smaller bits of fusible web for the smallest pieces. I worked on one block at a time to keep from getting all those small pieces mixed up.

2. Fold the 15" square in half diagonally and lightly press with an iron so you have a point of reference to place the stem and other appliqués. Place the stem and other appliqué pieces along the pressed fold.

3. Place the stem on the block background first. Place it 1/4" from both sides of the bottom corner, so when you sew the dark aqua corner pieces your stem is exactly in the middle. See diagram 1 from Pretty Petals quilt instructions.

4. Lay the large pieces of the appliqué on top of the stem. Place other pieces of appliqué that will be under the top layers, press and appliqué. (Like stems.) Cut away any background fabric from the back to eliminate bulk. Place the appliqué pieces on in layers, press and appliqué each layer.

"Happiness is to hold flowers in both hands"

Japanese Proverb

5. It's IMPORTANT to press the block between appliqué layers to keep block and appliqué lying as flat as possible. If using monofilament thread, BE CAREFUL to not over heat. The thread WILL melt! I like to lightly spray my block again after all the appliqué is on and press well.

6. TRIM blocks to measure 14 ¹⁄₂". This is where the 15" ruler will be SO helpful. Make sure you leave ¹⁄₄" at the corners for the points of your stems.

7. Appliqué all four blocks. Make sure you place the pointed stem ¹⁄₄" away from the bottom corner, so when you sew the blocks together you get a nice center point. (I picked mine out several times to get them right!) See diagram 1.

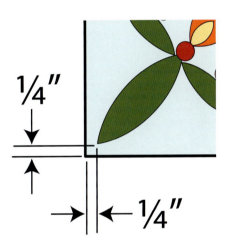

diagram 1

> Tip Appliqué largest piece (ie: brown piece before adhering yellow and red pieces on top.) Cut away background fabric from under brown. This will decrease the bulk with all the layers of appliqué.

8. Sew the 4 cream squares together, matching points of stems. Press seams open.

BORDERS

1. Sew 1 – 2 ¹⁄₂" x 28 ¹⁄₂" light green strip to top and bottom of quilt center. Press. See diagram 2.

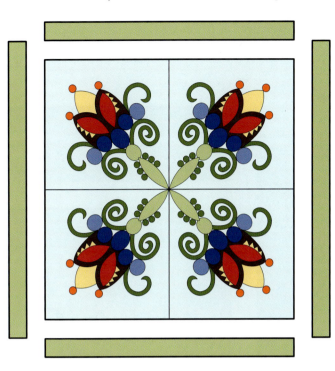

diagram 2

2. Sew 1 – 2 ¹⁄₂" x 32 ¹⁄₂" light green strip to sides of quilt center. Press.

3. Sew 1 – 4 ¹⁄₂" x 32 ¹⁄₂" medium blue strip to top and bottom of quilt center. Press. See diagram 3.

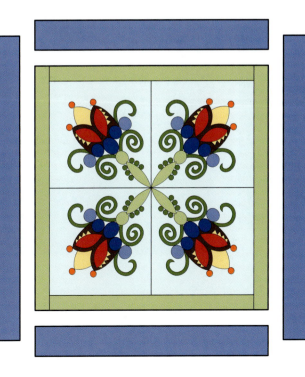

diagram 3

43

4. Sew 1 – 4 ½" x 40 ½" medium blue strip to sides of quilt center. Press.

5. Sew 1 – 6 ½" x 40 ½" blue floral strip to top and bottom of quilt. Press. See diagram 4.

6. Sew 1 – 6 ½" x 52 ½" blue floral strip to sides of quilt center. Press.

QUILT and ENJOY!

diagram 4

"Let us dance in the sun,
wearing wild flowers in our hair..."

Susan Polis Shutz

Kaleidoscope Quilt OPTIONS

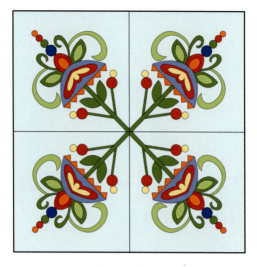

Sweet Pea

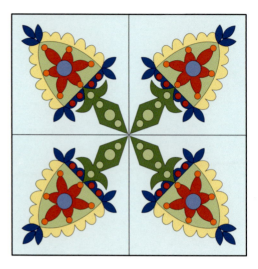

Marigold

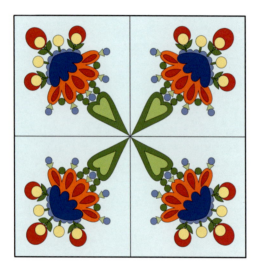

Daisy

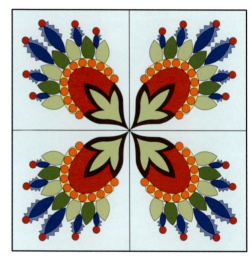

Zinnia

Rose

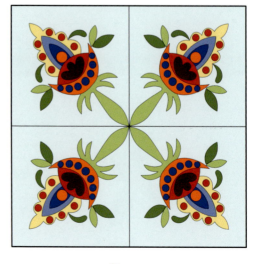

Poppy

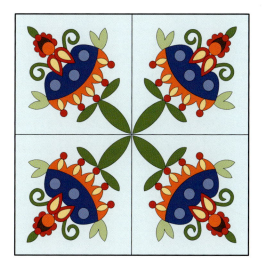

Bleeding Heart

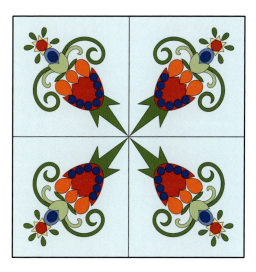

Geranium

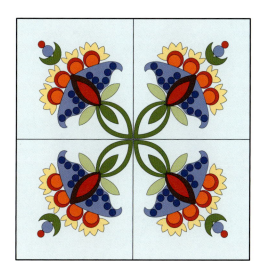

Sunflower

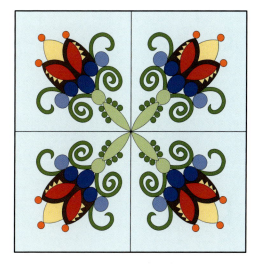

Iris

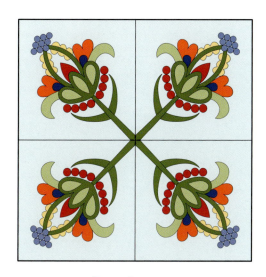

Snapdragon

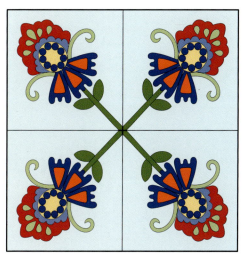

Carnation

RED POPPY GARDEN QUILT

RED POPPY GARDEN QUILT
Finished size: 70" x 70'
Designed by Sheri Howard
Quilted by Susan Hansen of Suzy Q's Quilts

When I needed another project for my book, I thought of a large red flower in a simple nine block grid. Since we already spent SO much time on the other quilts, I wanted to make one that was quick and easy. I added a scalloped border as a nice juxtaposition to the "squareness" of the quilt, plus the shape of the border is so "flower-like."

Fabric Requirements

White: 1 7/8 yards
Red with small white flowers: 1 1/2 yards
Red with large white flowers for last
    border: 1 5/8 yards
Binding: 7/8 yard
1 yard fusible web

APPLIQUÉ FABRIC:

Red polka dot: 1/3 yard
Medium spring green: 1/2 yard
Dark green: 1/4 yard
Yellow: fat quarter
Black for flower centers and binding: 1 yard

Cutting Instructions

All seams are 1/4" unless otherwise stated

From white cut:
3 – 12 1/2" strips WOF (width of fabric)
Subcut:
9 – 12 1/2" squares

6 – 4 1/2" strips WOF
Subcut:
2 – 4 1/2" x 44 1/2" strips. Set aside for later.
2 – 4 1/2" x 52 1/2" strips. Set aside for later.

From red with small white flowers cut:
9 – 2 1/2" strips WOF
Subcut:
6 – 2 1/2" x 12 1/2" strips
4 – 2 1/2" x 40 1/2"
2 – 2 1/2" x 44 1/2"

From red with large white flowers cut for last border:
6 – 9 1/2" strips WOF
Subcut:
2 – 9 1/2" x 52 1/2" strips
2 – 9 1/2" x 70 1/2" strips

Sewing Instructions

WHITE BORDER
1. For white border, sew 4 1/2" strips together end to end. Set aside for later.

APPLIQUÉ
1. Trace templates on page 92.

2. Place medium spring green leaves and dark green leaves on the block first and then the red polka dot flower. Press into place, and stitch appliqué pieces. Trim back of white background block to eliminate bulk. Press block. Place yellow center on red flower, press and stitch into place. Place black center on yellow, press and stitch into place. Spray lightly with fabric starch, press blocks well.

For sashing, red with small white flowers:
1. Sew 1 – 2 1/2" x 12 1/2" strip to one side of six appliquéd blocks. See diagram 1.

diagram 1

2. Sew blocks together in rows of 3, adding one appliquéd block to the right. See diagram 2.

diagram 2

3. Sew 1 – 2 1/2" x 40 1/2" strip to bottom of two block rows. See diagram 3.

diagram 3

4. Sew rows together and sew 1 – 2 ½" x 40 ½" strip to the top of block rows, and one on the bottom of block rows to make quilt center. See diagram 4.

5. Sew 1 – 2 ½" x 44 ½" strip to each side of quilt center. See diagram 4.

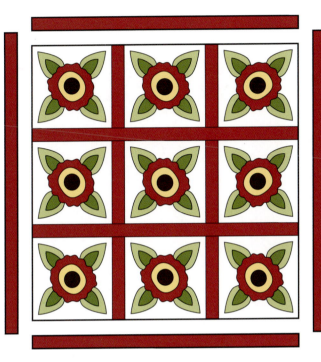

diagram 4

For white border:
1. Sew 1 – 4 ½" x 44 ½" strip to top and bottom of quilt center. See diagram 5.

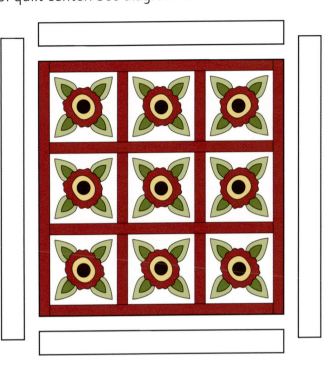

diagram 5

2. Sew 1 – 4 ½" x 52 ½" strip to each side of quilt center. See diagram 5.

For red with large white flower border:

1. Sew 1 – 9 ½" x 52 ½" strips to top and bottom of quilt center. See diagram 6.

2. Sew 1 – 9 ½" x 70 ½" strips to sides of quilt center. See diagram 6.

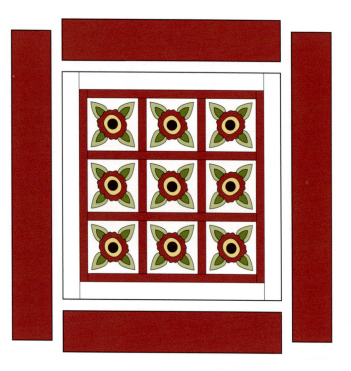

diagram 6

SCALLOPED EDGE:

Tip DO NOT mark scallop edge before your quilt is quilted. I like to have my machine quilter quilt to the edge of the square quilt. Then, mark the scalloped edge and cut along marked lines. See diagram 7.

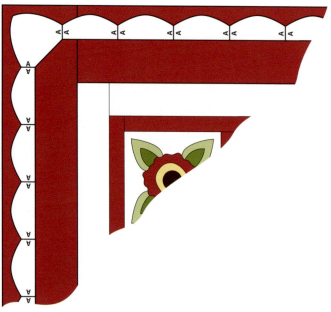

diagram 7

1. Bind quilt, turning softly at the corners of the scallops. Stop at the top of the corner points and make an angled mitered turn. Continue sewing around corner.

2. Binding measurement is based on 2 ½" strips. I cut the 2 ½" strips WOF, not on the bias. You can cut on the bias if you like, but there is enough "give" cutting the WOF across the grain, and it uses less fabric. You will need to plan on more fabric if you cut your strips on the bias.

QUILT and ENJOY!

"Summer set lip to

earth's bosom bare,

And left the flushed print

in a poppy there.

**Francis Thompson
"The Poppy," 1891**

" *Just living is not enough.*
One must have sunshine,
freedom, and a little flower."

Hans Christian Andersen

RED THROW PILLOW

RED THROW PILLOW
Finished size: 16" x 16"
Designed by Sheri Howard

If you do not have time for a large project but want to make some pretty petals, here is a fast throw pillow. Any of the Pretty Petals blocks could be used, however this one has its own design.

Fabric Requirements

White with small dots: 10 $\frac{1}{2}$" square
Small red stripe for border and back: $\frac{3}{4}$ yard
Muslin or scrap-backing for quilting top:
    fat quarter
Thin batting: 1 – 18" square

APPLIQUÉ PIECES
Scraps:
Yellow
Medium lime green
Dark green
Red
Medium blue
Orange

RICK-RACK
Royal blue – 1 package medium width
$\frac{1}{4}$ yard fusible web
1 – 16" pillow form

Cutting Instructions
All seams are $\frac{1}{4}$" unless otherwise stated.

From white with dots cut:
1 – 10 $\frac{1}{2}$" square

From red stripe cut:
2 – 4" strips WOF (width of fabric)
Subcut:
2 – 4" x 10 $\frac{1}{2}$" strips
2 – 4" x 17 $\frac{1}{2}$" strips

For pillow backs cut:
1 – 9" x 16 $\frac{1}{2}$"
1 – 12" x 16 $\frac{1}{2}$"

Sewing Instructions

APPLIQUÉ:
Trace templates on page 94.

Place green stems under yellow flower on the white with dots 10 $\frac{1}{2}$" square and press into place, then appliqué. See diagram 1. Trim away white dots fabric from back to eliminate bulk. Place red center on yellow flower, press and appliqué. Trim away yellow from back to eliminate bulk. Place medium blue center on red, press and appliqué. Place orange center on medium blue, press and appliqué. Spray lightly with starch and press.

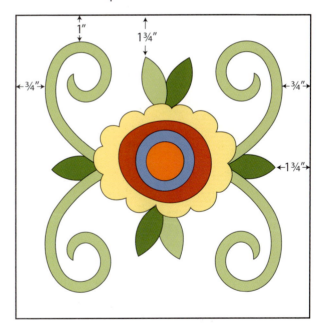

diagram 1

For red borders:
1. Sew 1 – 4" x 10 $\frac{1}{2}$" strip to top and bottom of white center. Press seams toward red.

2. Sew 1 – 4" x 17 $\frac{1}{2}$" strip to each side of white center. Press seams toward red.

QUILTING THE TOP:

1. Layer pillow top with a piece of batting and muslin. Quilt pillow top. Trim top, batting and muslin so pillow top measures 16 ½" x 16 ½".

2. Sew rick-rack around the white block on the seam line.

PILLOW BACK:

1. Stitch a narrow hem along one 16 ½" side of both back pieces. See diagram 2.

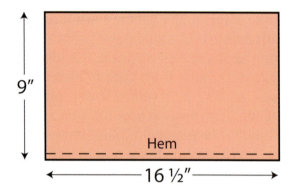

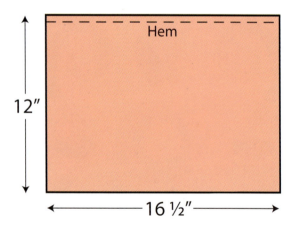

diagram 2

2. Lay 9" x 16 ½" on top of 12" x 16 ½" piece, overlapping hemmed edges, right sides up. Making the back piece to measure 16 ½" x 16 ½". See diagram 3. Pin pieces together.

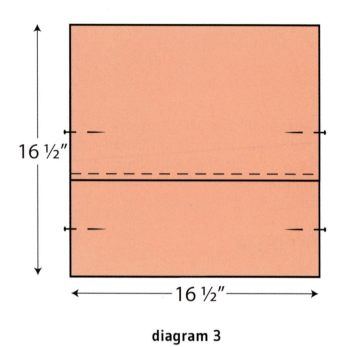

diagram 3

3. Lay quilted pillow top on the back, right sides together. Sew around entire 16 ½" square, back stitching where pieces overlap for extra security when pillow form is inserted.

4. Clip corners.

5. Turn pillow inside out. Press.

6. Insert pillow form.

"I perhaps owe having become a painter to flowers."

Claude Monet

"When you have only two
pennies left in the world,
buy a loaf of bread with one,
and a lily with the other."

Chinese Proverb

MARKET BAG

MARKET BAG
Finished size: 13" x 14"
Designed by Sheri Howard

I am not too fond of those unattractive reusable bags that you get at the store. A quilter needs her own appliquéd Pretty Petals bag—don't you think? Pretty bags seem to make the cost of living not so painful after you write out the check! Happy shopping!

Fabric Requirements

Lime green: ²/₃ yard
Lining fabric: ¹/₂ yard
Dark green: 3" x 18"
Red for bow: ¹/₆ yard or 2 pieces 5 ¹/₂" x 18 ¹/₂"
Royal blue: ¹/₄ yard
Green, yellow scraps for appliqué
¹/₄" yard fusible web
4 – 1" buttons

Cutting Instructions
All seams are ¹/₄" unless otherwise stated

From lime green cut:
2 – 14" x 16" for outside bag
2 – 4" x 21 ¹/₂" for handles

From lining fabric cut:
2 – 14" x 16"

From red cut:
2 pieces using bow template
8 circles for flower center using template

From royal blue cut:
1 – 3" x 36" strip for binding trim
8 flower petals using template

From green and yellow scraps cut:
3 green stems using template (cut 2 reversed)
1 yellow flower center using template

Sewing Instructions

APPLIQUÉ:

Templates can be found on pages 95–96.

1. Lay the flower petal pieces, stems and yellow center on one of the lime green 14" x 16" pieces. See photo and diagram 1. When you are happy with the placements, remove the stems and yellow center. Press and appliqué just the flower petals.

diagram 1

2. Lay the stems and yellow center appliqué pieces on top of the flower petals. Press and appliqué into place. Press lightly.

3. Position the red dots on the yellow center. Press and appliqué .

BAG AND LINING:

1. Sew bag pieces right sides together along the two 16" sides and along one 14" side. See diagram 2. Repeat the same for the lining. Press all seams open on bag and lining.

diagram 2

2. Match side seam and bottom seam of the bag and stitch 3" from the bottom point. See diagram 3. This makes a nice pleat on the bottom so your bag will sit flat. Trim point off to $1/2$" from stitching line. See diagram 4. Repeat for bag lining.

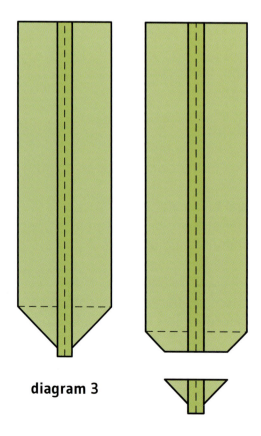

diagram 3

diagram 4

3. Turn bag inside out. Leave the lining wrong side out. Place the lining down inside the bag, wrong sides together, matching up the top edges. Baste bag and lining together along the top edge. You will be finishing the top edge like binding on a quilt.

BAG TOP BINDING:

1. Measure the bag opening.

2. Cut the royal blue binding strip that measurement plus 1" for seam. Sew 3" ends together using a $^1/_2$" seam to form a circle. Press seam open. Fold wrong sides together lengthwise and press. Pin the binding strip to the lining (inside of bag) and measure so it fits the bag opening. If needed, adjust your $^1/_2$" seam to make a perfect fit.

3. Make sure you are sewing on the lining side, sew binding strip to bag using a $^1/_4$" seam. Press seam toward binding. Bring binding to the front of the bag pin and top stitch along the edge, around the entire bag opening.

HANDLES:

1. With right sides together, sew along the long side of the handle strips and across one short end using a $^1/_4$" seam. Turn handle inside out. Press under the raw edges of the short end $^1/_4$". This opening will be stitched closed when you top stitch the handle to the bag.

2. Lay the handle 2 $^1/_2$" from the side seam of bag. See diagram 5. Pin handle into place on front of bag, and pin the same side of the handle on the back of the bag 2 $^1/_2$" from the side seam.

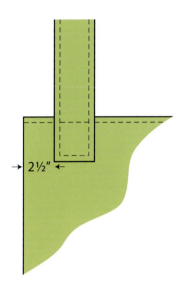

2½"

diagram 5

3. Top stitch around the entire handle stitching the opening closed as you go. Then, go back and sew a square around the ends of the handle for security. See diagram 5.

4. Repeat for second handle.

5. Hand sew buttons on the ends of the handles, inside the sewn square.

BOW:

1. Stitch bow pieces right side together using a ¼" seam around the entire piece, leaving a 4" opening along one long side.

2. Clip corners. Turn inside out.

3. Press a ¼" seam inside on the 4" where you turned the bow. Top stitch around the entire bow, stitch the opening closed as you go.

4. Tie your bow one of the front handles.

ENJOY your shopping!

Tip Start with the knotted thread under the button so you don't have any unsightly knots on the inside of your bag. Knot off under the button.

> "I wandered lonely as a cloud
> That floats on high o'er vales and hills,
>   When all at once I saw a crowd,
> A host, of golden daffodils;
>   Beside the lake, beneath the trees,
> Fluttering and dancing in the breeze
>   Continuous as the stars that shine
>   And twinkle on the milky way,
> They stretched in never-ending line
>   Along the margin of a bay:
> Ten thousand saw I at a glance,
> Tossing their heads in sprightly dance."

William Wordsworth
"I Wandered Lonely as a Cloud," 1804

*"I want it said of me by those
who knew me best,
that I always plucked a thistle
and planted a flower
where I thought a flower
would grow."*

Abraham Lincoln

Acknowledgements

It takes MANY people to put together a quilt book like this. First and foremost I want to thank the Kansas City Star for the opportunity to publish my floral designs. Thank you Diane McLendon and Doug Weaver for your faith in my work.

Of course my editor Kent Richards for his tireless work in deciphering my notes and making my crazy ideas sound intelligent. Thank you so much!

To Bob Deck the designer for putting together all the information into an attractive and exciting book! Your talents are appreciated.

Thank you to Jo Ann Groves for making the pictures look so lovely and tech editor Jane Miller for her diligence in reading and correcting the directions. I am so grateful.

Eric Sears—thank you for the fabulous illustrations. I absolutely love the Kaleidoscope blocks, your illustrations really help make the book feel the way I had envisioned it.

A special thank you to Aaron Leimkuehler for shooting photos out in the rain all day. You said it was the first photo shoot you ever did in the rain—I hope it is your last. You were so willing to go the extra mile. The pictures are so beautiful. You know I love your work!

Thank you to RileyBlake Fabrics for their incredible gingham fabric featured in the Pretty Petals quilt.

To Moda Fabrics for their generous fabrics featured in the Pretty Petals and Kaleidoscope quilts.

Thank you to Marcus Fabrics for the beautiful red fabrics in the Red Poppy Garden quilt.

What would we do without our quilters? I believe a quilt top is pretty before it is quilted, but AMAZING after the quilter works her magic. Thank you Sheri Bear and Susan Hansen.

Thank you to my husband Cody, who is my biggest fan and is always so supportive in my quilting endeavors. I said in my other books that he is a "quilter's dream"— he truly is!

Finally, this book would not have its beautiful photos were it not for Bob and Jamie Bradley from Rigby, Idaho and their impeccable 2.5 acres of garden. You know the kind of summer garden you see in magazines and would love to have, but don't want to take care of? That is how beautiful their place is. It is a shame that we can show so little of it! You were so darling to stand out in the rain the entire day, help with all the set up and take down, and bring us hot chocolate. THANK YOU SO MUCH!

Templates

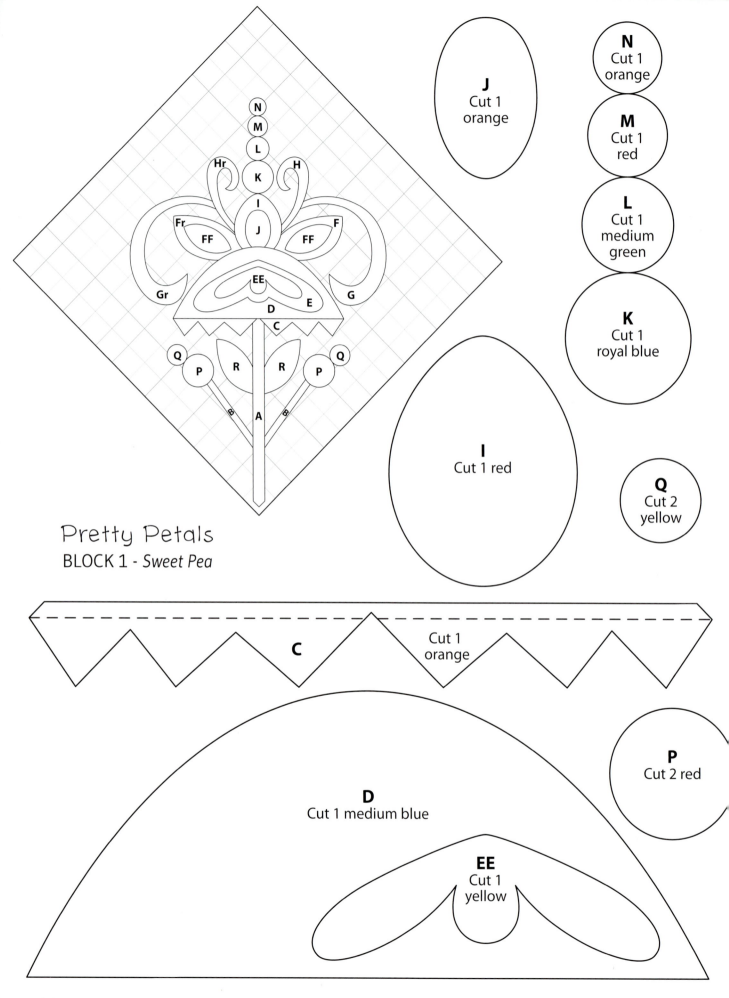

J Cut 1 orange

N Cut 1 orange

M Cut 1 red

L Cut 1 medium green

K Cut 1 royal blue

I Cut 1 red

Q Cut 2 yellow

Pretty Petals
BLOCK 1 - *Sweet Pea*

C Cut 1 orange

P Cut 2 red

D Cut 1 medium blue

EE Cut 1 yellow

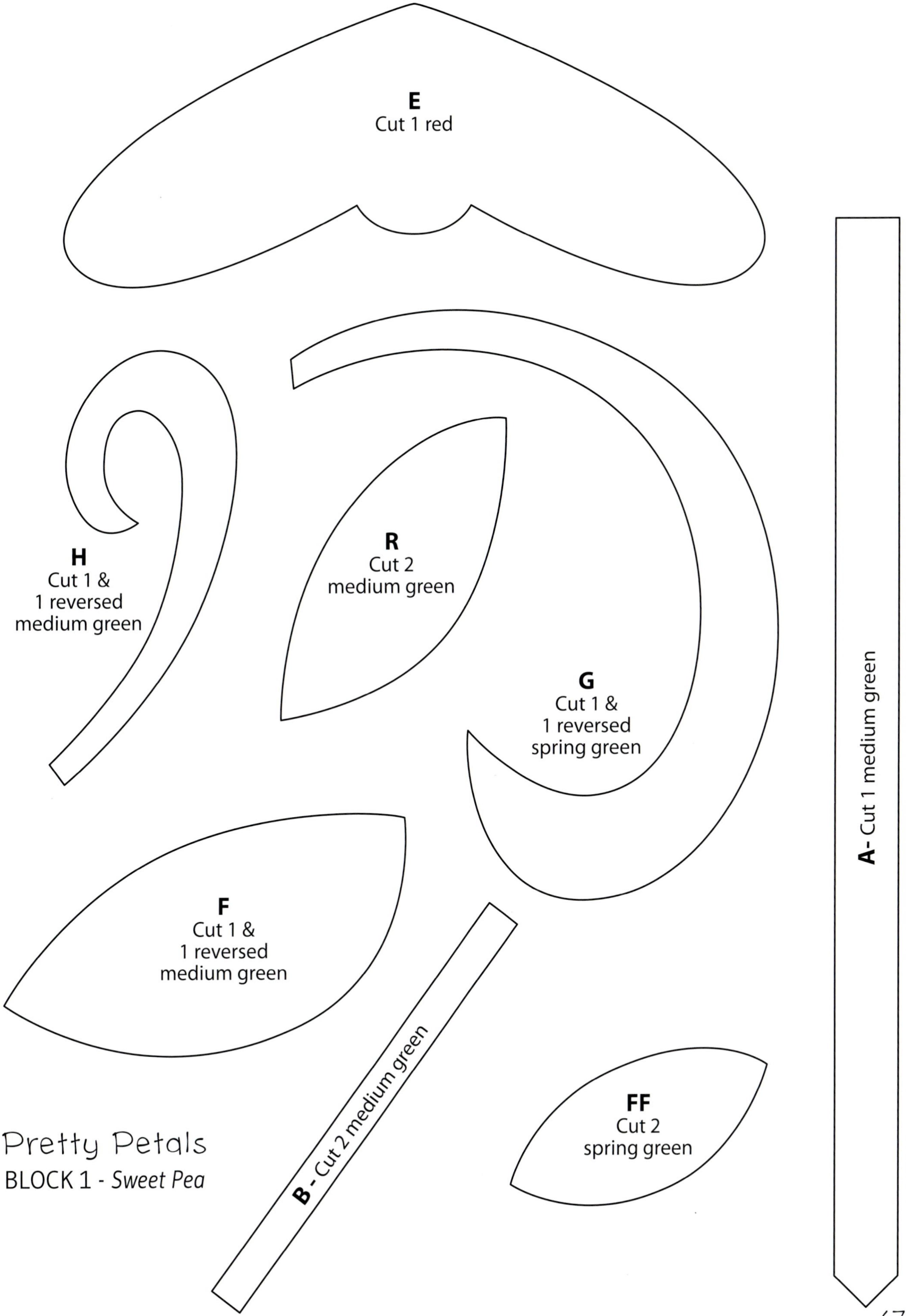

E
Cut 1 red

H
Cut 1 &
1 reversed
medium green

R
Cut 2
medium green

G
Cut 1 &
1 reversed
spring green

A - Cut 1 medium green

F
Cut 1 &
1 reversed
medium green

B - Cut 2 medium green

FF
Cut 2
spring green

Pretty Petals
BLOCK 1 - *Sweet Pea*

J
Cut 1
royal blue

I
Cut 6
royal blue

G
Cut 6
orange

K
Cut 1
spring green

A
Cut 1
medium green

JJ
Cut 3
spring green

H
Cut 1 &
1 reversed
yellow

Pretty Petals
BLOCK 2 - *Marigold*

Pretty Petals
BLOCK 2 - *Marigold*

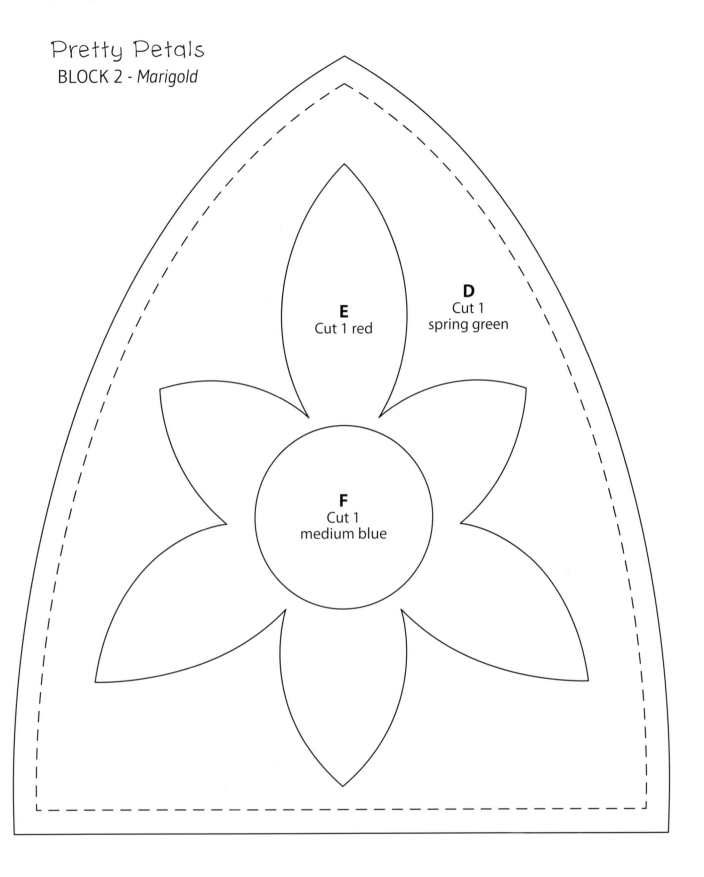

E
Cut 1 red

D
Cut 1
spring green

F
Cut 1
medium blue

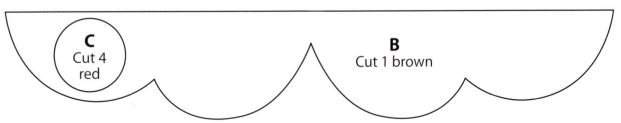

C
Cut 4
red

B
Cut 1 brown

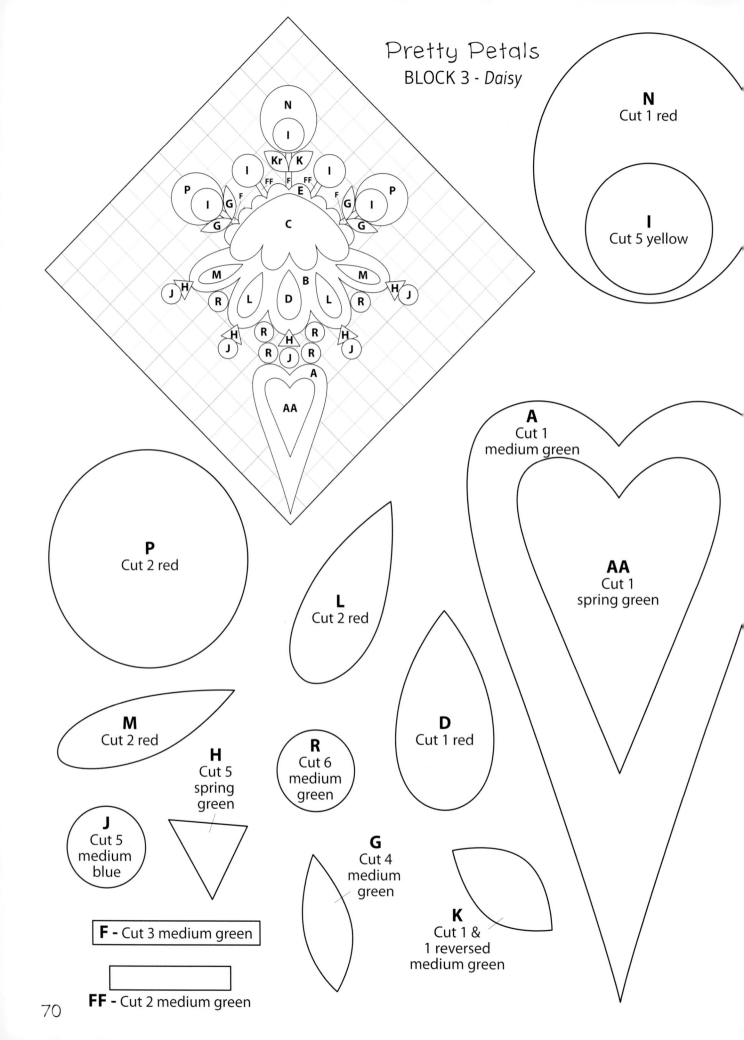

Pretty Petals
BLOCK 3 - *Daisy*

N
Cut 1 red

I
Cut 5 yellow

P
Cut 2 red

L
Cut 2 red

A
Cut 1
medium green

AA
Cut 1
spring green

D
Cut 1 red

M
Cut 2 red

H
Cut 5
spring
green

R
Cut 6
medium
green

J
Cut 5
medium
blue

G
Cut 4
medium
green

K
Cut 1 &
1 reversed
medium green

F - Cut 3 medium green

FF - Cut 2 medium green

70

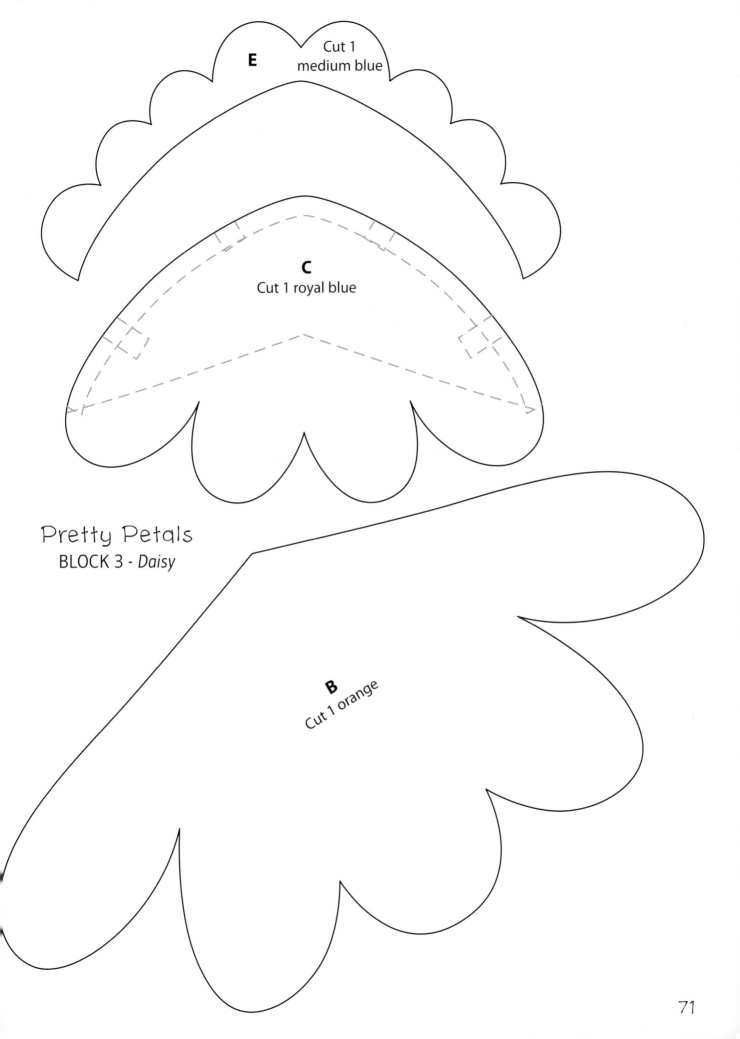

E
Cut 1
medium blue

C
Cut 1 royal blue

Pretty Petals
BLOCK 3 - *Daisy*

B
Cut 1 orange

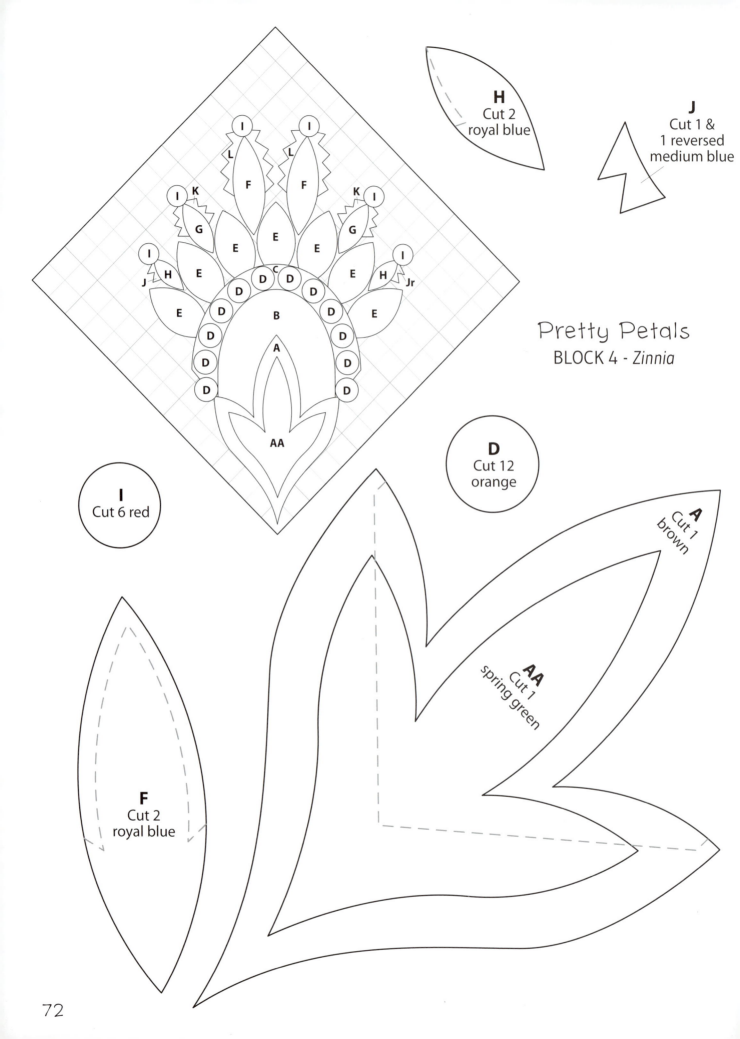

H
Cut 2
royal blue

J
Cut 1 &
1 reversed
medium blue

Pretty Petals
BLOCK 4 - *Zinnia*

D
Cut 12
orange

I
Cut 6 red

A
Cut 1
brown

AA
Cut 1
spring green

F
Cut 2
royal blue

Pretty Petals
BLOCK 4 - Zinnia

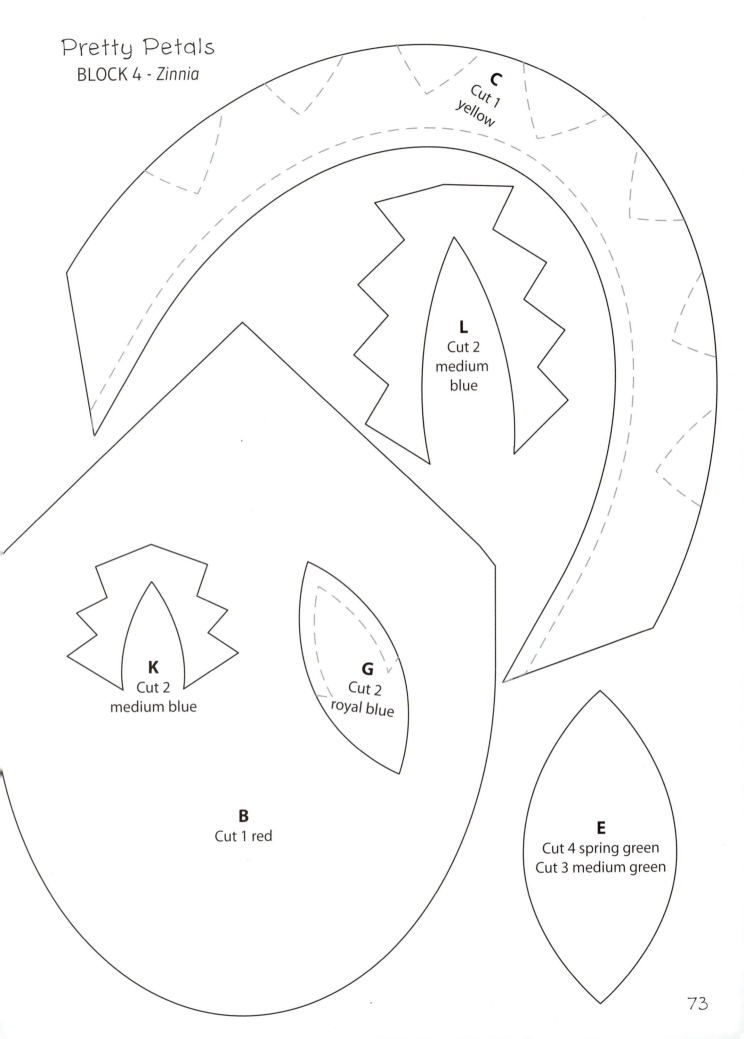

C
Cut 1
yellow

L
Cut 2
medium
blue

K
Cut 2
medium blue

G
Cut 2
royal blue

B
Cut 1 red

E
Cut 4 spring green
Cut 3 medium green

Pretty Petals
BLOCK 5 - *Rose*

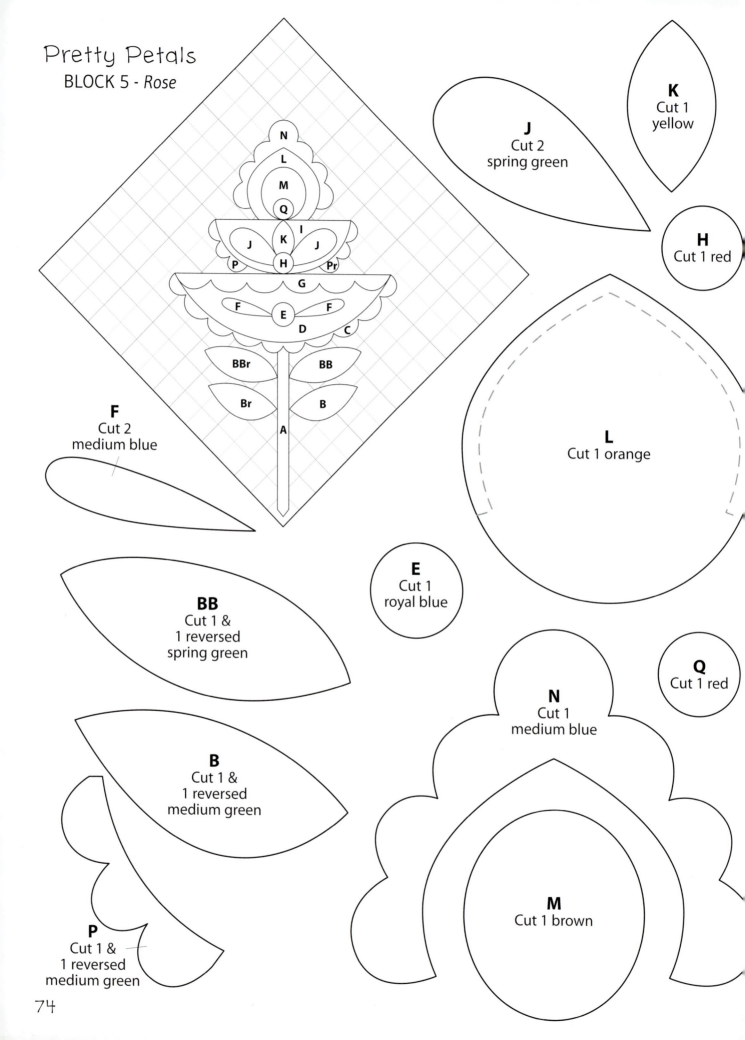

N
Cut 1
medium blue

M
Cut 1 brown

Q
Cut 1 red

J
Cut 2
spring green

K
Cut 1
yellow

H
Cut 1 red

L
Cut 1 orange

E
Cut 1
royal blue

F
Cut 2
medium blue

BB
Cut 1 &
1 reversed
spring green

B
Cut 1 &
1 reversed
medium green

P
Cut 1 &
1 reversed
medium green

74

Pretty Petals
BLOCK 5 - *Rose*

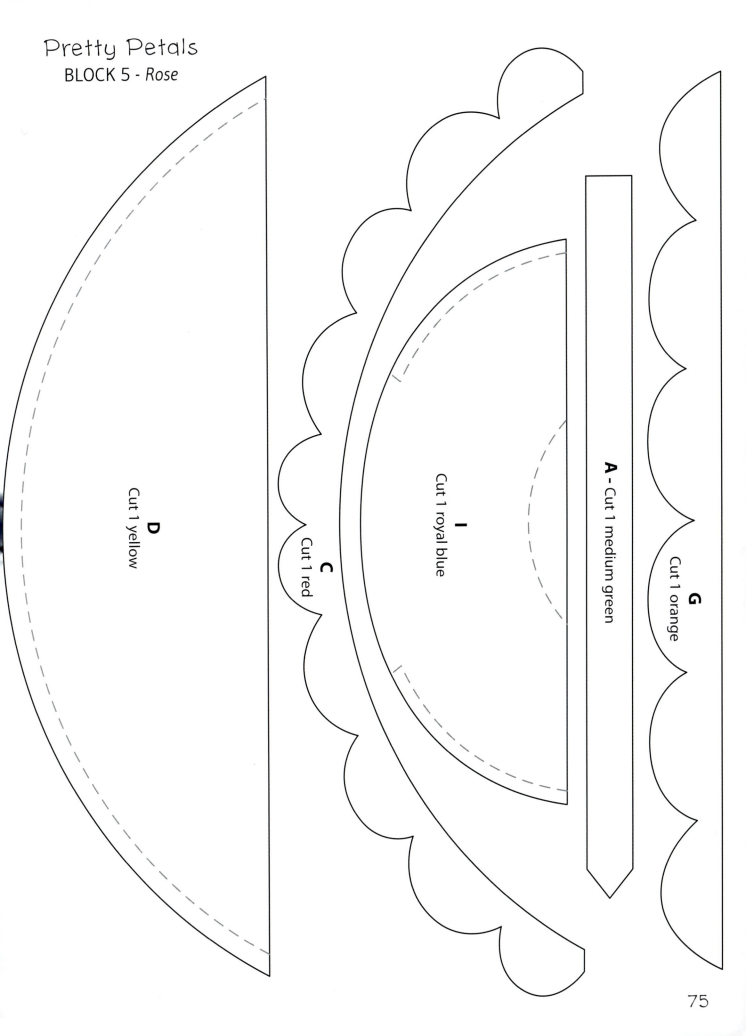

D
Cut 1 yellow

C
Cut 1 red

I
Cut 1 royal blue

A - Cut 1 medium green

G
Cut 1 orange

Pretty Petals
BLOCK 6 - *Poppy*

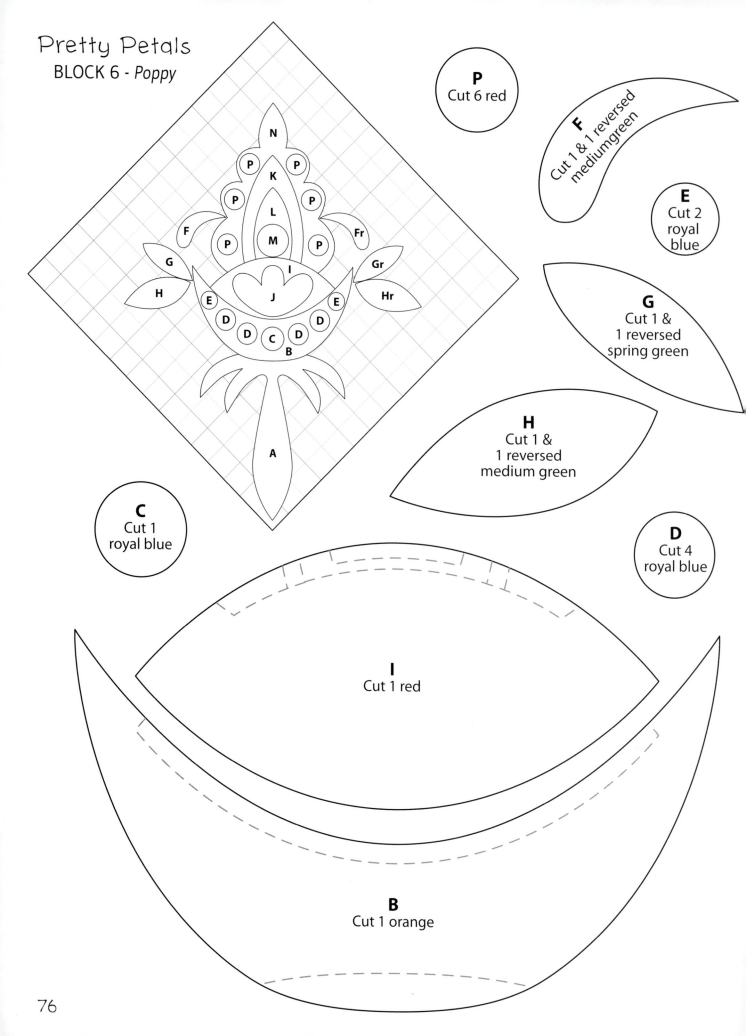

P
Cut 6 red

F
Cut 1 & 1 reversed
medium green

E
Cut 2
royal
blue

G
Cut 1 &
1 reversed
spring green

H
Cut 1 &
1 reversed
medium green

C
Cut 1
royal blue

D
Cut 4
royal blue

I
Cut 1 red

B
Cut 1 orange

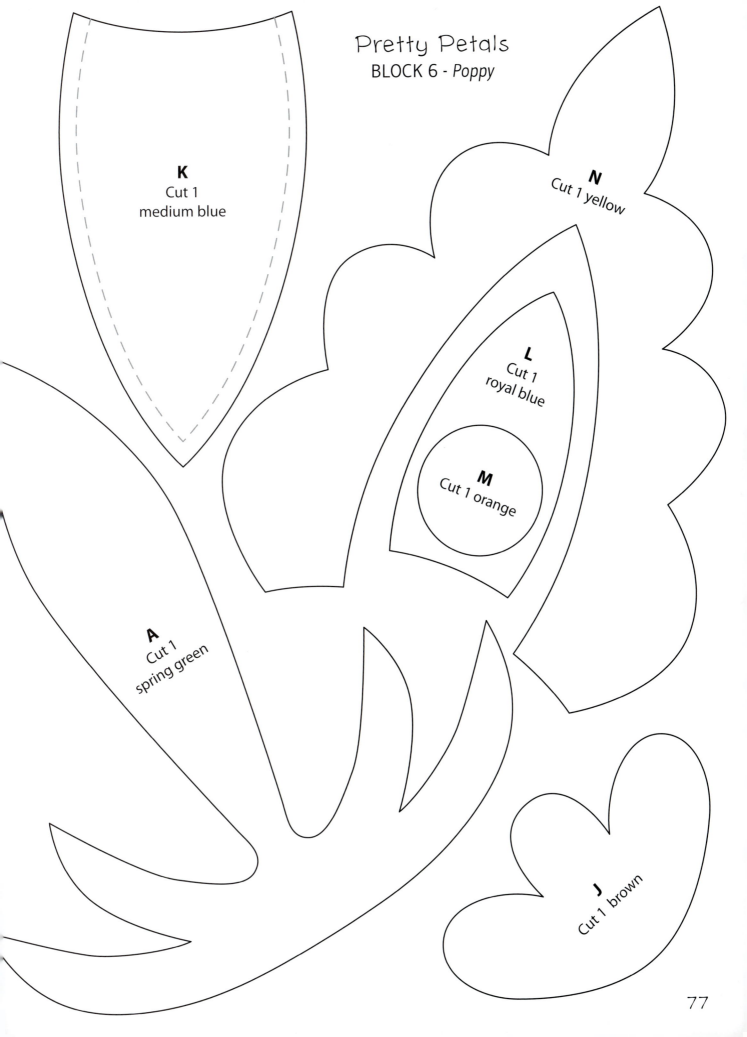

Pretty Petals
BLOCK 6 - *Poppy*

K
Cut 1
medium blue

N
Cut 1 yellow

L
Cut 1
royal blue

M
Cut 1 orange

A
Cut 1
spring green

J
Cut 1 brown

77

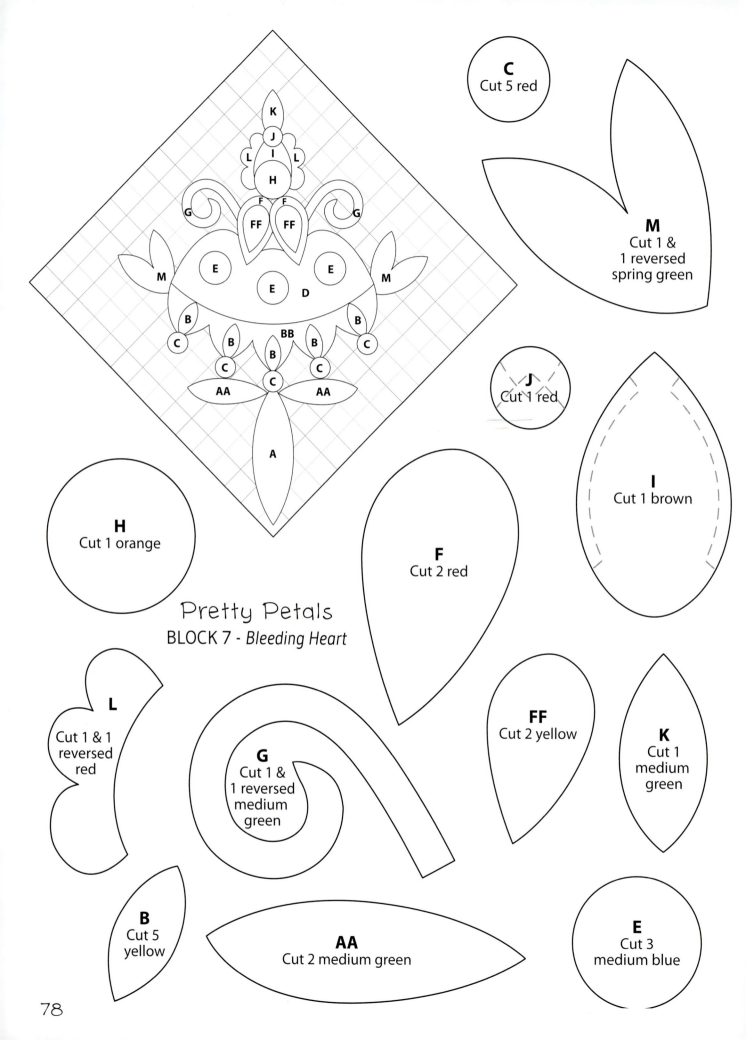

C
Cut 5 red

M
Cut 1 &
1 reversed
spring green

J
Cut 1 red

I
Cut 1 brown

H
Cut 1 orange

Pretty Petals
BLOCK 7 - *Bleeding Heart*

F
Cut 2 red

L
Cut 1 & 1
reversed
red

G
Cut 1 &
1 reversed
medium
green

FF
Cut 2 yellow

K
Cut 1
medium
green

B
Cut 5
yellow

AA
Cut 2 medium green

E
Cut 3
medium blue

Pretty Petals
BLOCK 7 - *Bleeding Heart*

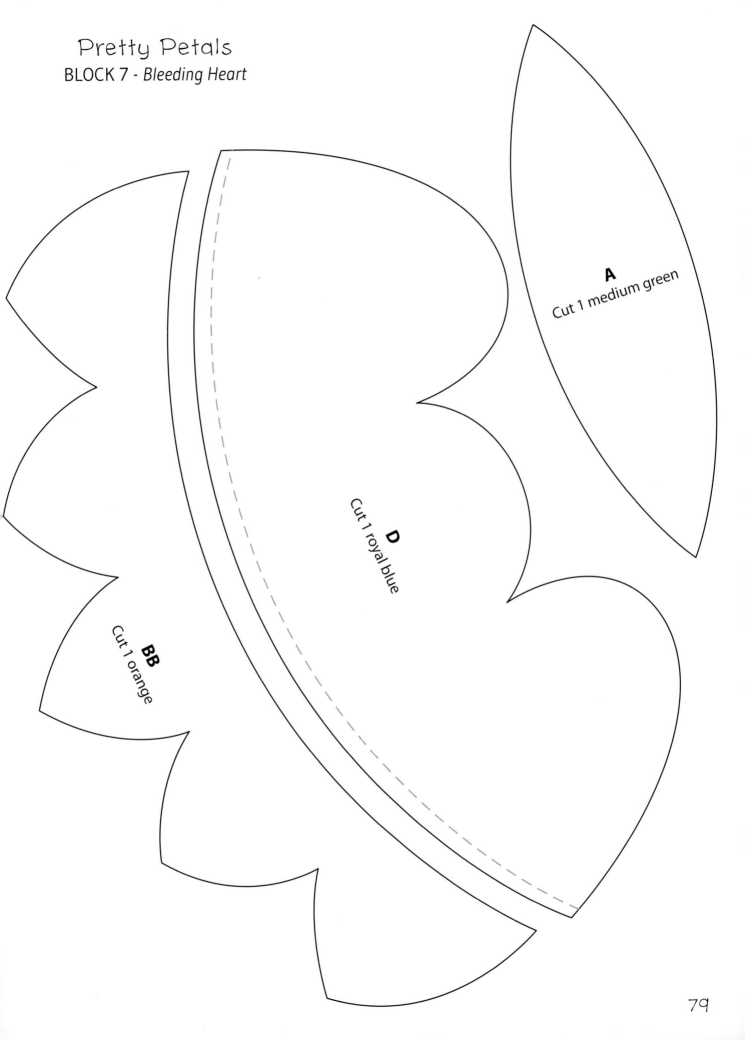

A
Cut 1 medium green

D
Cut 1 royal blue

BB
Cut 1 orange

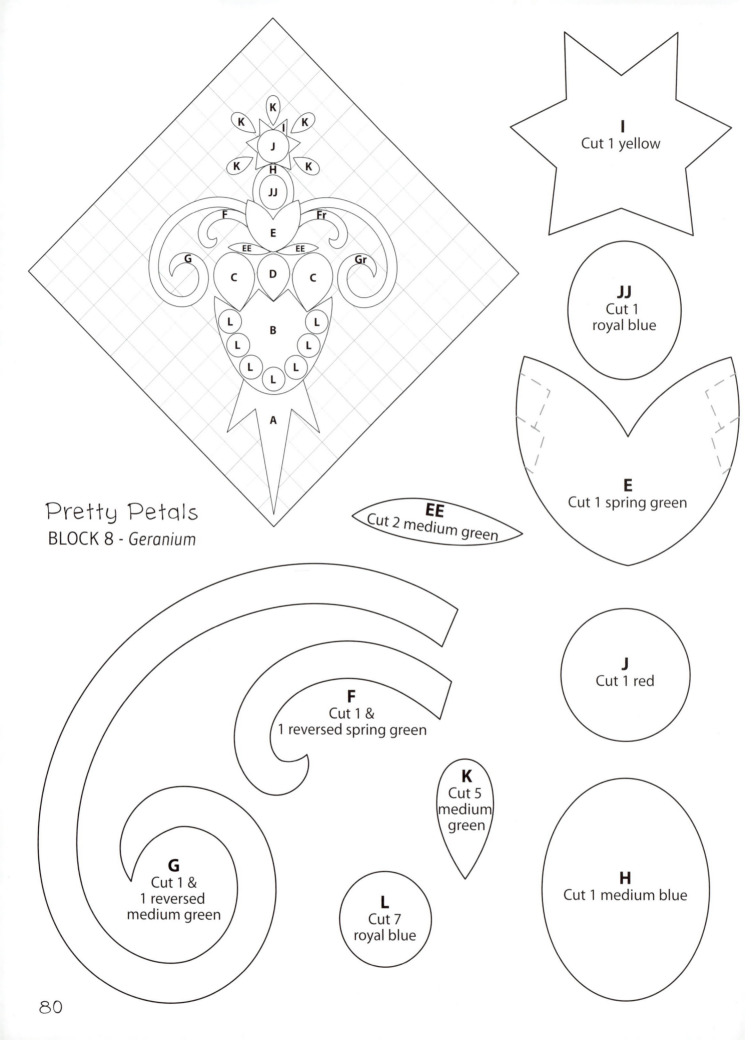

I
Cut 1 yellow

JJ
Cut 1
royal blue

E
Cut 1 spring green

Pretty Petals
BLOCK 8 - *Geranium*

EE
Cut 2 medium green

F
Cut 1 &
1 reversed spring green

J
Cut 1 red

K
Cut 5
medium
green

G
Cut 1 &
1 reversed
medium green

L
Cut 7
royal blue

H
Cut 1 medium blue

80

Pretty Petals
BLOCK 8 - *Geranium*

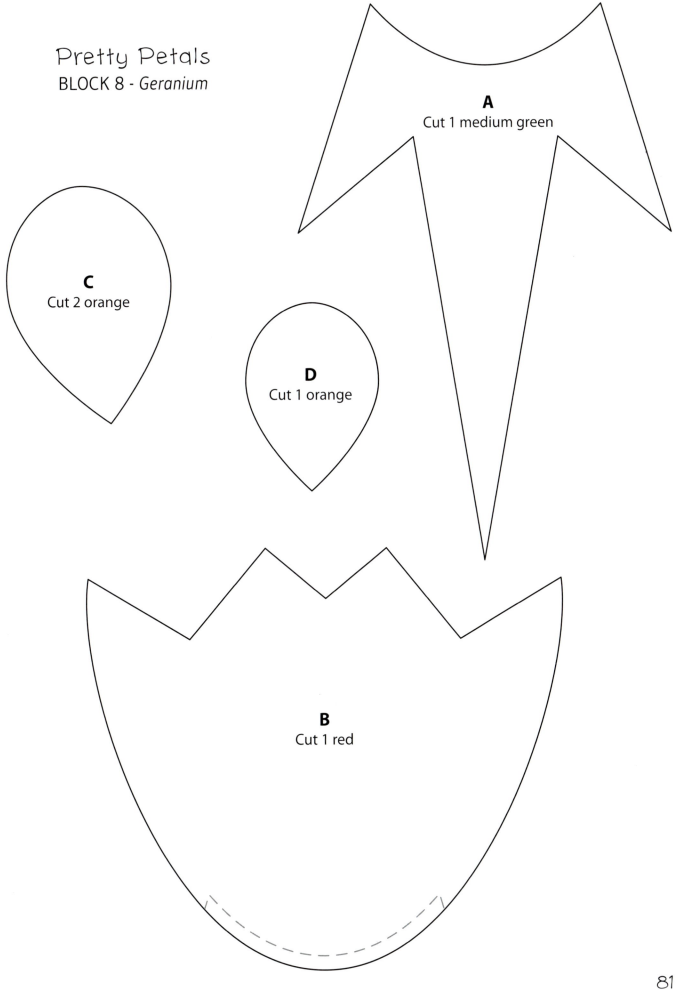

A
Cut 1 medium green

C
Cut 2 orange

D
Cut 1 orange

B
Cut 1 red

81

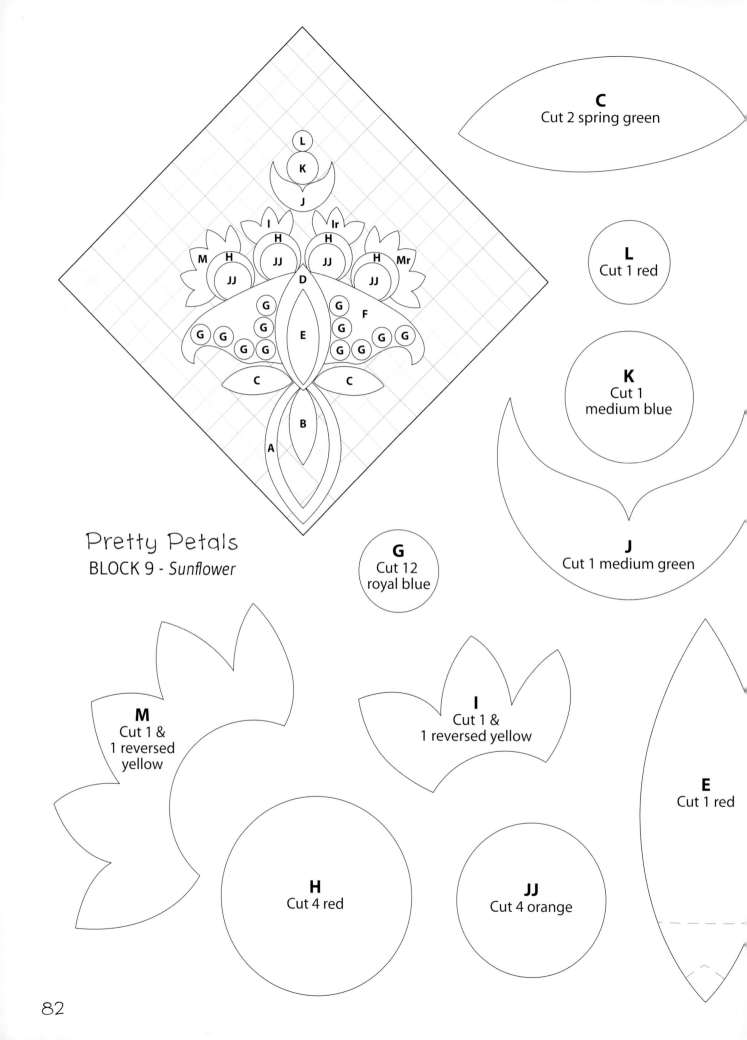

C
Cut 2 spring green

L
Cut 1 red

K
Cut 1
medium blue

J
Cut 1 medium green

G
Cut 12
royal blue

Pretty Petals
BLOCK 9 - *Sunflower*

M
Cut 1 &
1 reversed
yellow

I
Cut 1 &
1 reversed yellow

H
Cut 4 red

JJ
Cut 4 orange

E
Cut 1 red

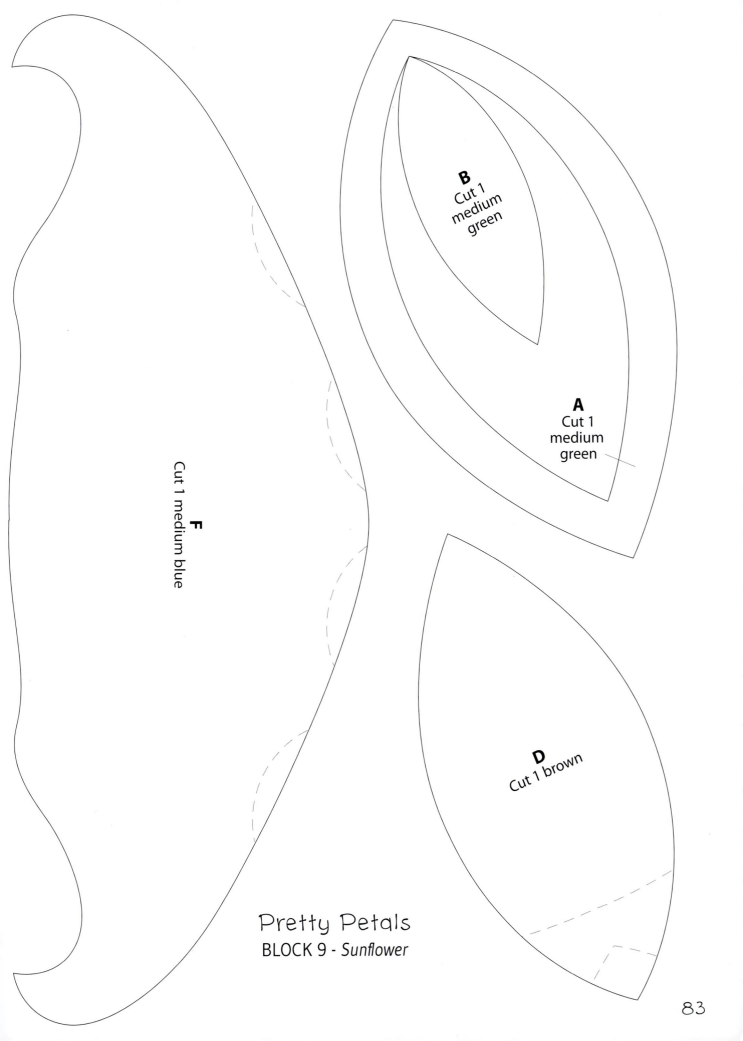

B
Cut 1
medium
green

A
Cut 1
medium
green

F
Cut 1 medium blue

D
Cut 1 brown

Pretty Petals
BLOCK 9 - *Sunflower*

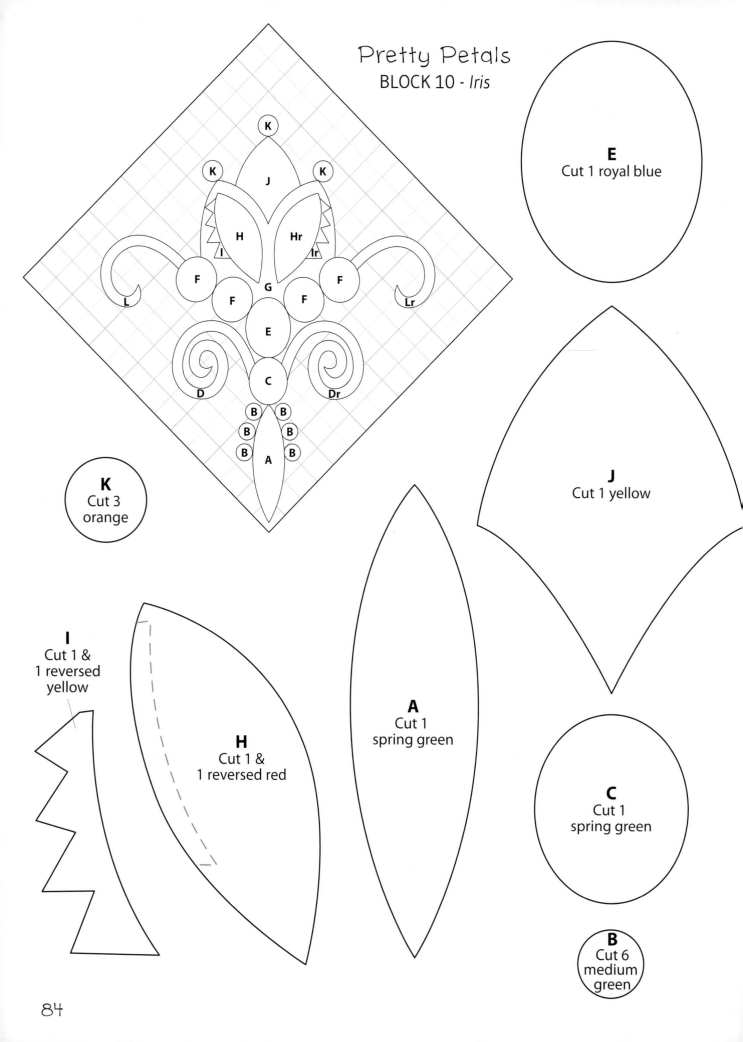

Pretty Petals
BLOCK 10 - *Iris*

E
Cut 1 royal blue

K
Cut 3
orange

J
Cut 1 yellow

I
Cut 1 &
1 reversed
yellow

H
Cut 1 &
1 reversed red

A
Cut 1
spring green

C
Cut 1
spring green

B
Cut 6
medium
green

84

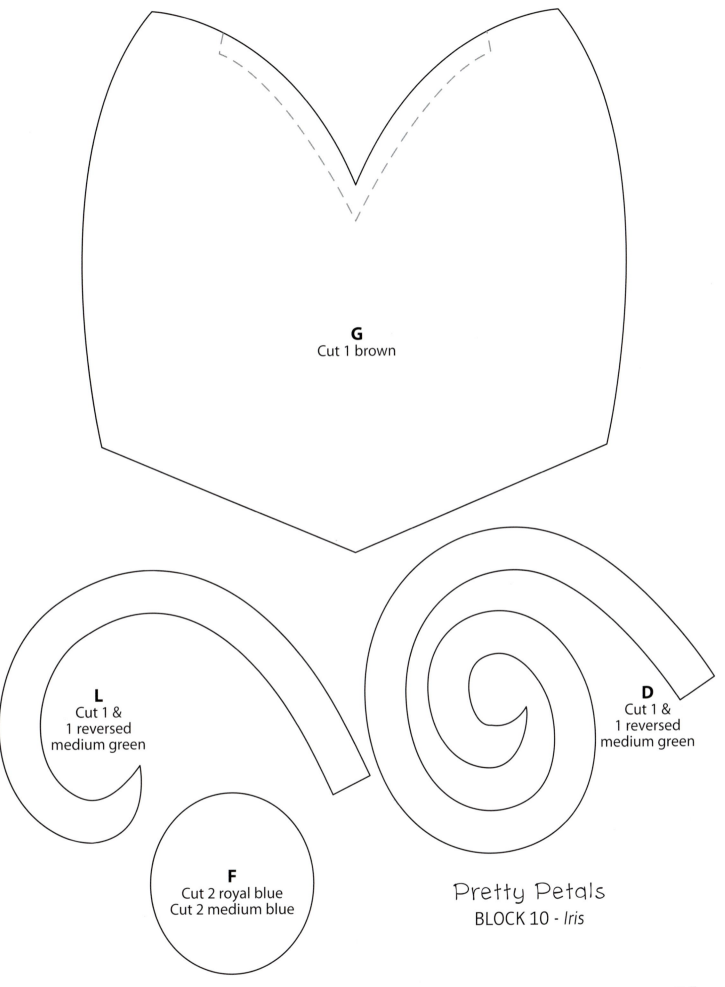

G
Cut 1 brown

L
Cut 1 &
1 reversed
medium green

D
Cut 1 &
1 reversed
medium green

F
Cut 2 royal blue
Cut 2 medium blue

Pretty Petals
BLOCK 10 - *Iris*

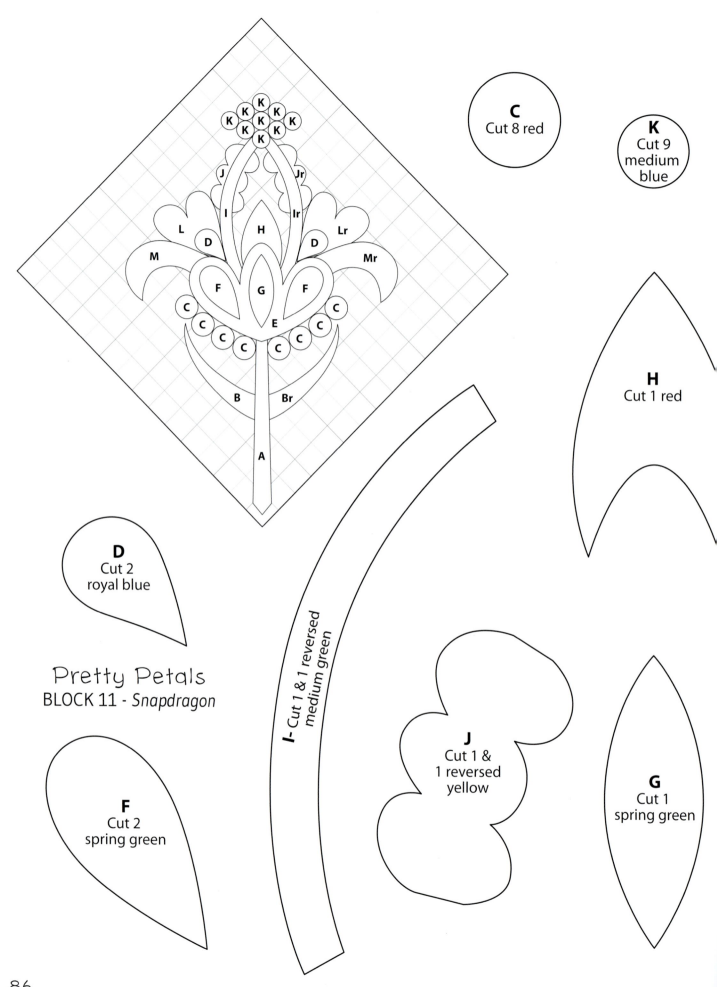

C
Cut 8 red

K
Cut 9
medium
blue

H
Cut 1 red

D
Cut 2
royal blue

Pretty Petals
BLOCK 11 - *Snapdragon*

I - Cut 1 & 1 reversed
medium green

J
Cut 1 &
1 reversed
yellow

G
Cut 1
spring green

F
Cut 2
spring green

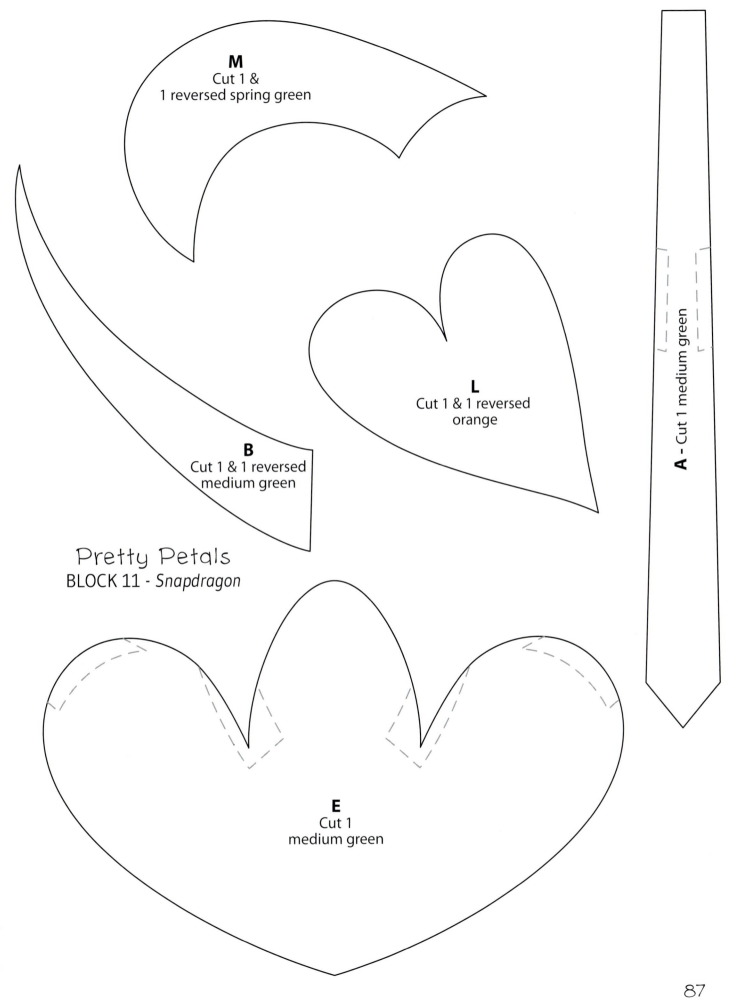

M
Cut 1 &
1 reversed spring green

L
Cut 1 & 1 reversed
orange

B
Cut 1 & 1 reversed
medium green

A - Cut 1 medium green

Pretty Petals
BLOCK 11 - *Snapdragon*

E
Cut 1
medium green

Pretty Petals

BLOCK 12 - *Carnation*

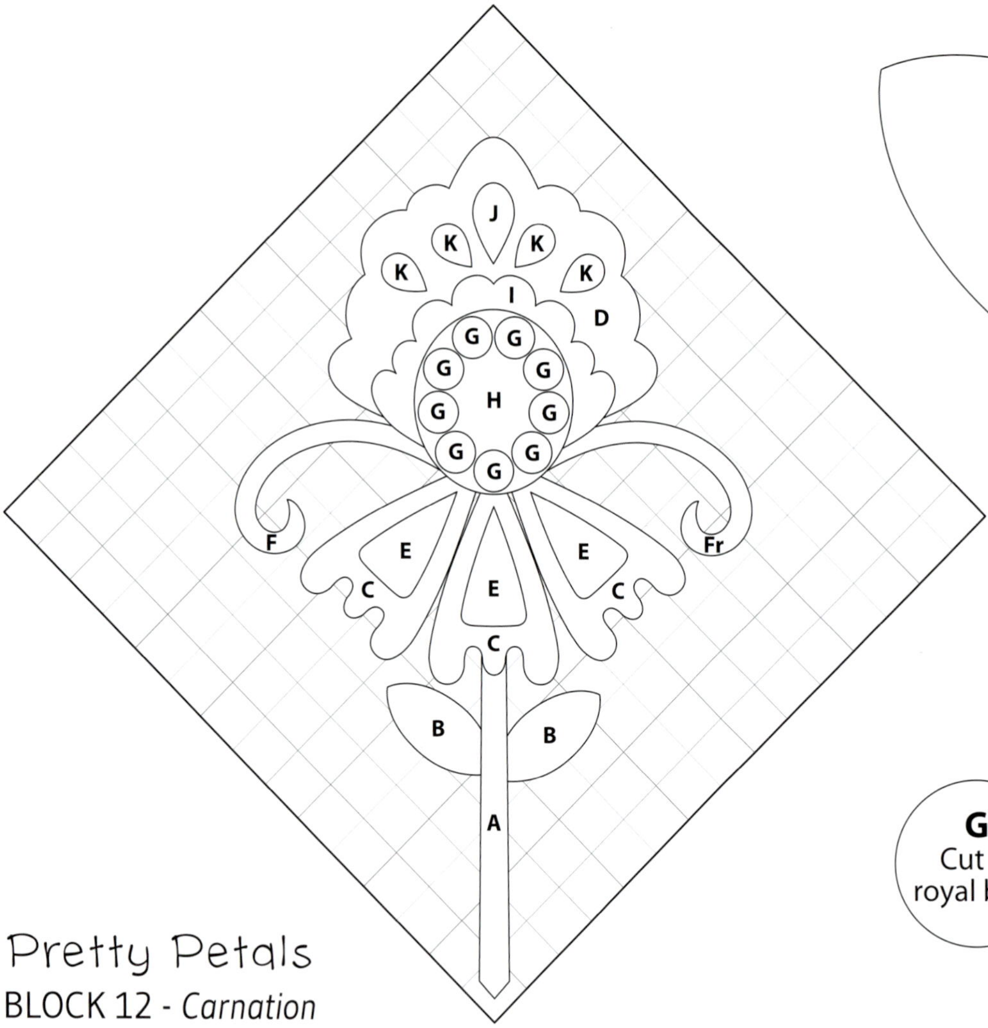

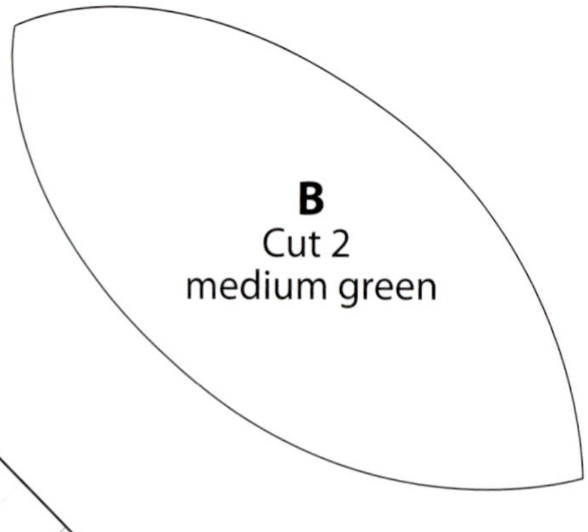

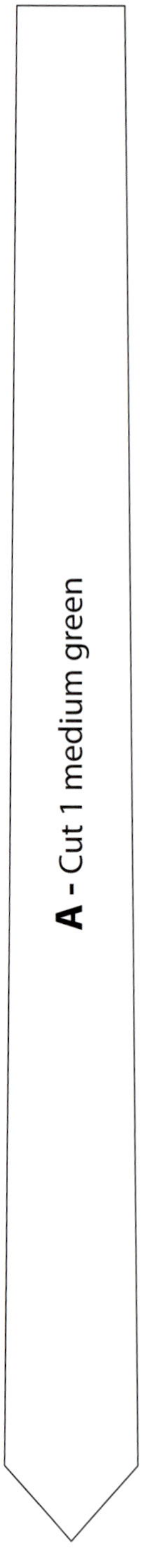

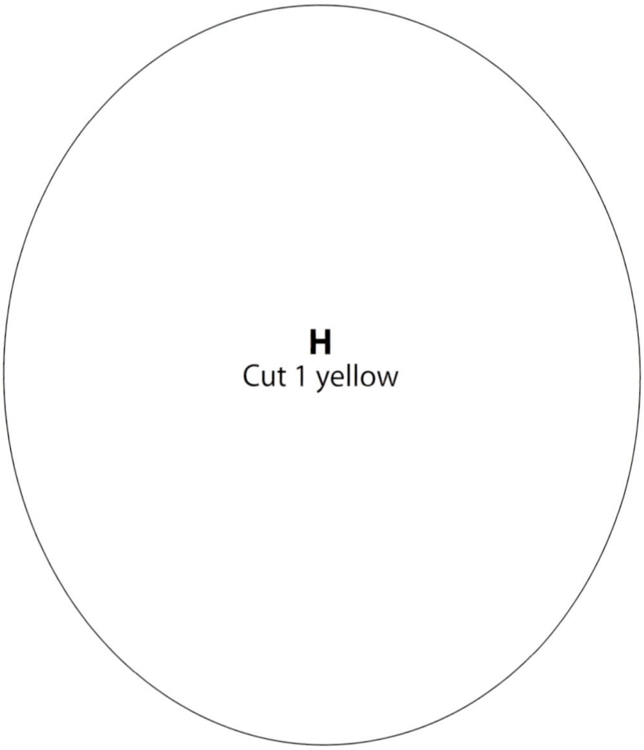

J
K
K
K
K
I
D
G
G
G
G
G
H
G
G
G
G
G
F
Fr
E
E
E
C
C
C
B
B
A
G
Cut 9
royal blue

B
Cut 2
medium green

A - Cut 1 medium green

H
Cut 1 yellow

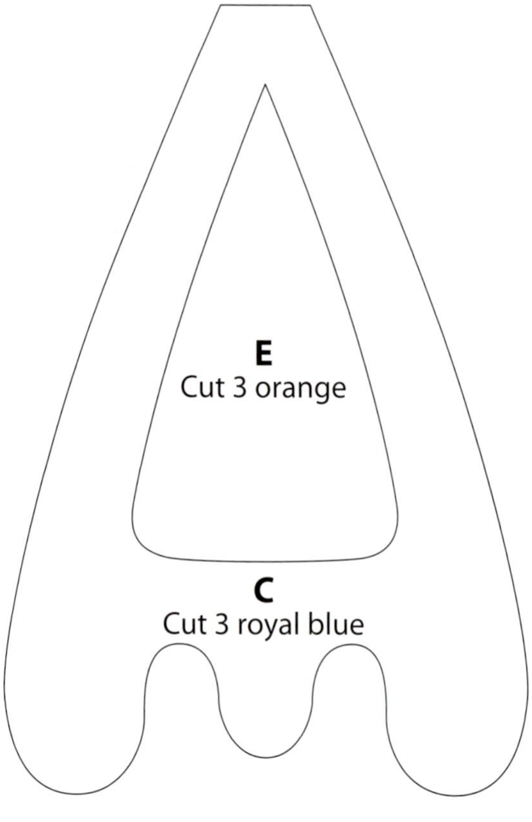

E
Cut 3 orange
C
Cut 3 royal blue

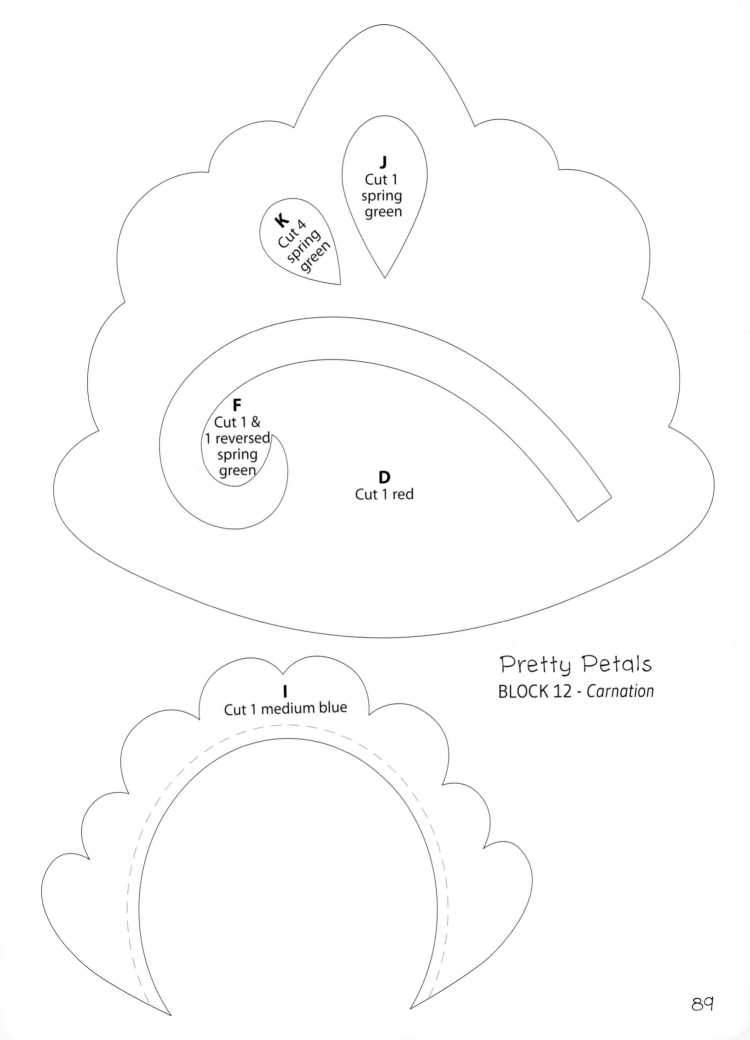

J
Cut 1
spring
green

K
Cut 4
spring
green

F
Cut 1 &
1 reversed
spring
green

D
Cut 1 red

Pretty Petals
BLOCK 12 - *Carnation*

I
Cut 1 medium blue

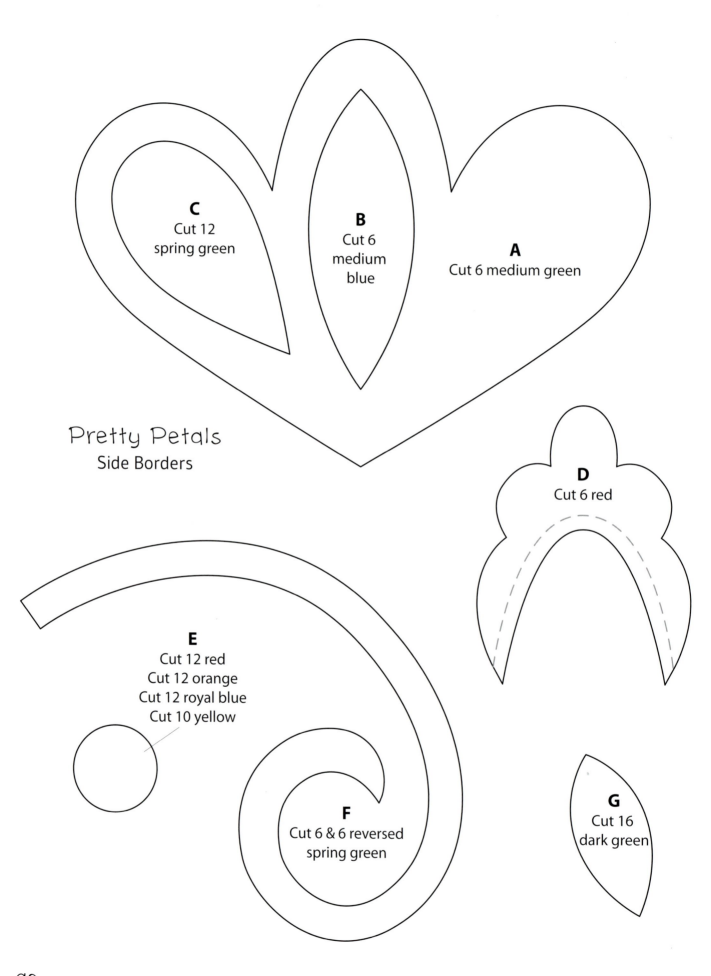

C
Cut 12
spring green

B
Cut 6
medium
blue

A
Cut 6 medium green

Pretty Petals
Side Borders

D
Cut 6 red

E
Cut 12 red
Cut 12 orange
Cut 12 royal blue
Cut 10 yellow

F
Cut 6 & 6 reversed
spring green

G
Cut 16
dark green

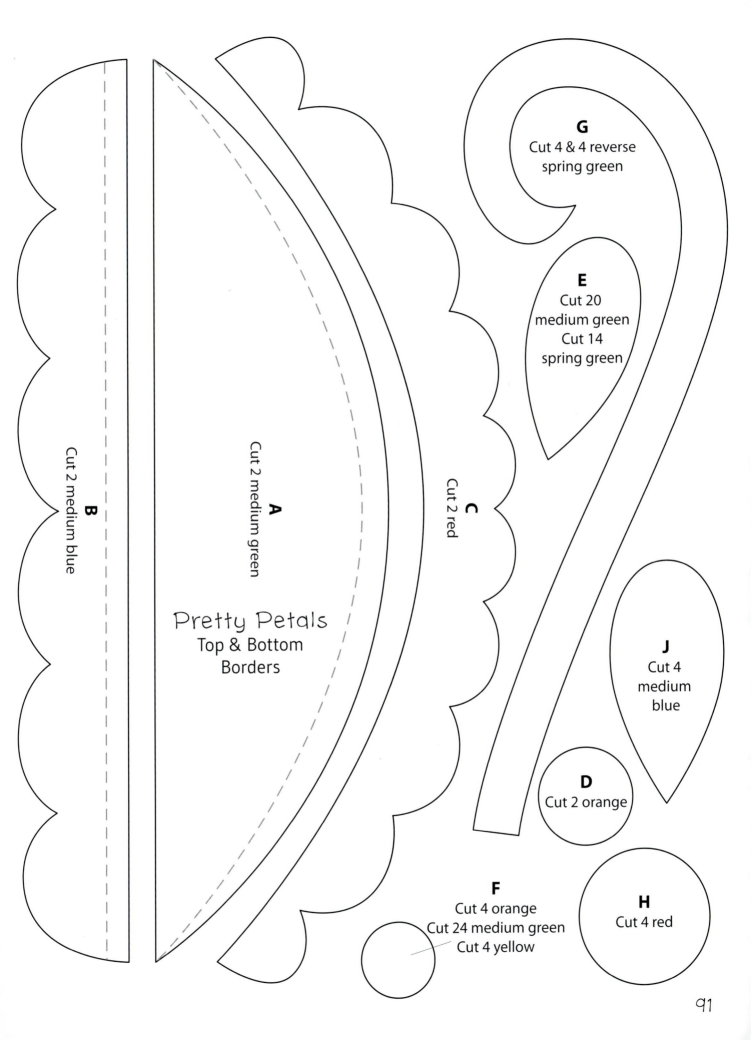

G
Cut 4 & 4 reverse
spring green

E
Cut 20
medium green
Cut 14
spring green

B
Cut 2 medium blue

A
Cut 2 medium green

Pretty Petals
Top & Bottom
Borders

C
Cut 2 red

J
Cut 4
medium
blue

D
Cut 2 orange

F
Cut 4 orange
Cut 24 medium green
Cut 4 yellow

H
Cut 4 red

91

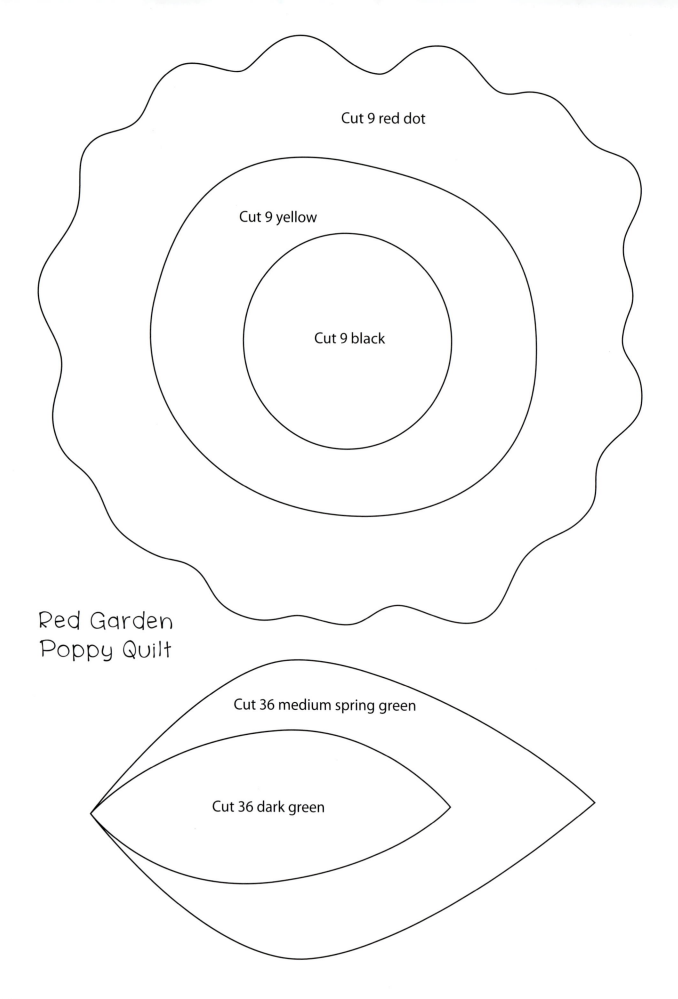

Cut 9 red dot

Cut 9 yellow

Cut 9 black

Red Garden
Poppy Quilt

Cut 36 medium spring green

Cut 36 dark green

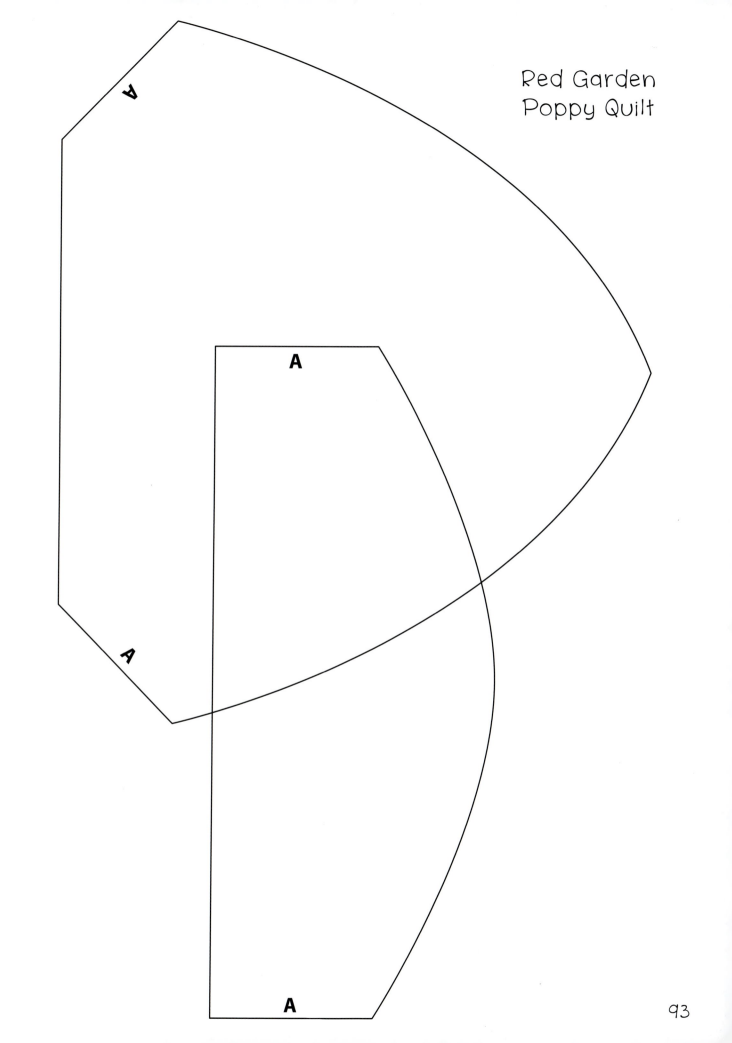

Red Garden
Poppy Quilt

A

A

A

A

93

Cut 1 yellow

Cut 1 red

Cut 1 blue

Cut 1 orange

Red Throw Pillow

Cut 4 dark green
Cut 2 medium green

Cut 2 & 2 reverse
medium green

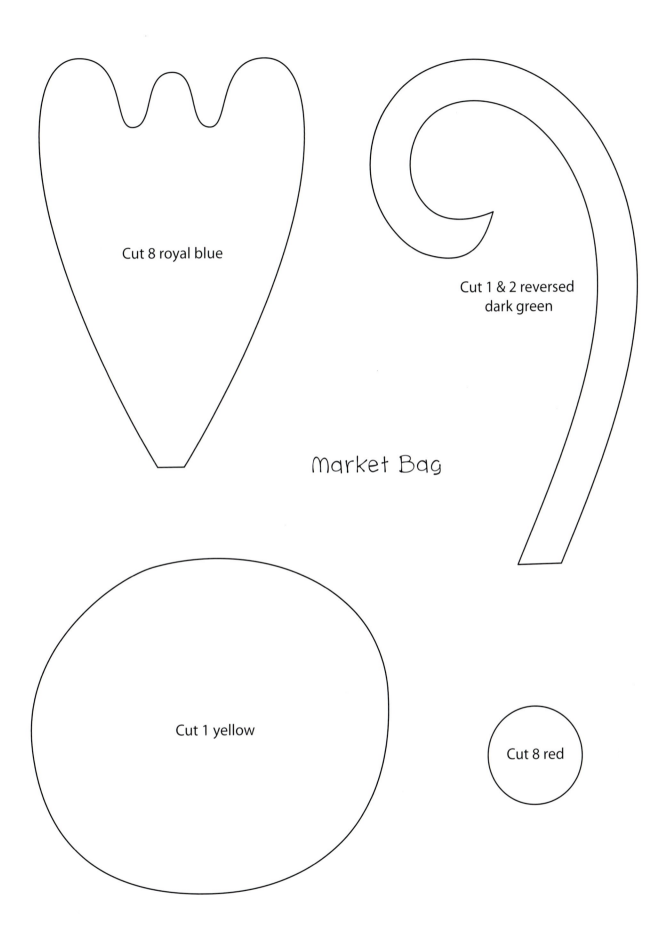

Cut 8 royal blue

Cut 1 & 2 reversed
dark green

Market Bag

Cut 1 yellow

Cut 8 red

Market Bag

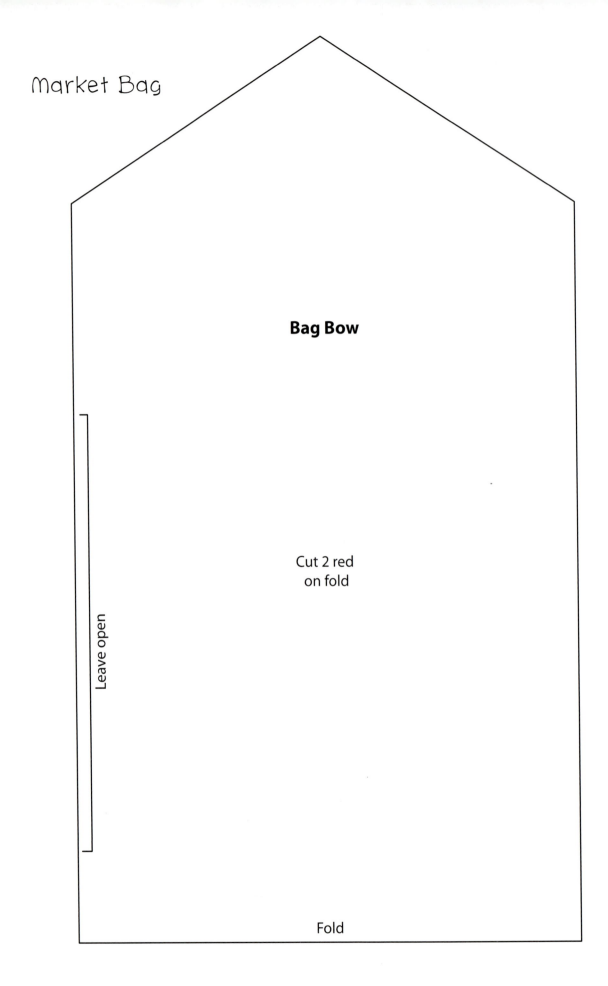

Bag Bow

Cut 2 red
on fold

Leave open

Fold